My Now for the

College Grad

My Now for the
College Grad

Moovin4ward Publishing
Huntsville, Alabama

Copyright 2013 Moovin4ward Publishing

Library of Congress Control Number: 2013917950

ISBN: Paperback   978-0-9910227-00
        eBook   978-0-9910227-17

Printed in the United States of America

All rights reserved. No part of this publication may be reproduced, stored in a retrieval system or transmitted in any form or by any means, electronic, mechanical, photocopying, recording or otherwise, without the written permission of the publisher.

Publisher:
   Moovin4ward Publishing
   A Division of Moovin4ward Presentations LLC
   www.Moovin4ward.com

Contents

Part 1: Here Now 7

- Now What? 9
- Dealing Positively with Adversity 19
- Dear Younger Sibling: 29
- Not Another J.O.B.! 45
- So You Finished... Now What? 55
- A Knot Between the Educational Sector and Living a Meaningful Life 65

Part 2: Moving Forward 77

- Go Swim in the Ocean: The Butterfly Syndrome 79
- Keep On Rolling! 87
- Moving Without the Ball 97
- Success! How Bad Do You Want It? 109
- Preparation for Excellence: A 5 Step Process 117

Part 3: Future Success 129

- If the Shoe Fits 131
- Congratulations on Finishing: You Are Now at the Starting Line 141
- Work Ethic: What You Put In Is What You Get Out 153
- Personal Branding: Achieve Your Full Potential! 167
- MENglish and WOMENglish 179
- Increase Your Impact, Influence, and Income with the Power of Stories 191

My Now...

...for the College Grad

Part 1: Here Now

My Now...

Frank Simmons

Frank Simmons, Jr. is a speaker, trainer, coach, mentor, author, and motivator. Frank has traveled extensively throughout the United States speaking to audiences of all ages and backgrounds.

He worked for Monster Worldwide as a Speaker, Trainer, Area Manager, Content Contributor, providing national speaker training and coaching and speaking to high school, college students, parents, and staff. He also spoke for organizations such as Bank of America, the Equal Employment Opportunity Council, Army ROTC, and others.

Frank is the Chief Inspirational Officer for Frankly Speaking Seminars providing workshops, seminars, coaching, training, and keynotes. Frank is the author and co-author of 4 books - The Man of Destiny, Unleash the Greatness Within You, Pursue IT with All You've Got, and My Vision, My Plan, My Now. He is also a National Trainer for Time To Teach, Moovin4ward Presentations, Rachel's Challenge, and The Art Institutes.

With over 25 years of speaking, coaching, and training experience, Frank is well equipped to help you, your company, or your organization achieve your goal of speaking publicly.
He has presented to over a million people across the United States and has trained, coached, and mentored over 1000 professional speakers, coaches, singers, clergy, and business professionals.

...for the *College Grad*

Now What?

Frank Simmons

One of my favorite movies of all times is Finding Nemo. I just think that it was a great movie. Nemo, after being caught by a dentist who was scuba diving, finds himself in the dentist's fish tank in his office. He, of course, is scared to death. There is one fish in the tank named Gill who was the only other fish who ever lived in the ocean. He was always devising a plan to escape to the ocean. At the end of the movie we see that one of Gill's escape plans had finally worked. One of the last scenes shows Gill and the other fish in plastic bags floating in the water. One of the questions they asked Gill was Now What? They had escaped but, now they were in plastic bags floating and not swimming freely. Gill had been so focused on the escape that he had no plans of what to do once they got out. Now let's talk about you.

You have just come to the end of what was a very long and sometimes tedious journey that began when you were 5 or 6 years old. It has been somewhere between a 17 to 20 year journey of what we call formal education and NOW it's over. NOW what? Some of you just exhaled and some of you just tensed up. Either way – NOW it is time to make some decisions and take some action. But, before we do that, let's

My Now...

take a look at what's going on. Let me take a stab and see if I can pinpoint where you are right NOW.

Some of you thought that you would never get into college. There were circumstances that limited your belief that a college education was a possibility. You may have come from a broken home with only one parent that struggled to make ends meet. Maybe one of your parents died at an early age and you struggled with the loss of love. It could have been that you had a learning disability that damaged your self-esteem and made you feel less than. Some of you grew up in dangerous neighborhoods where you thought you could not escape drugs, gangs, or prostitution. Maybe you had teachers that made you feel like you had no options. No one in your family had ever been to college and maybe you didn't get the support that you needed to consider college.

But, on the other hand, some of you never had a doubt that college was in your future. You came from well-established homes with a legacy of college graduates. You grew up with both of your parents at home. Maybe you didn't have everything but, you had enough. The neighborhood you grew up in was awesome. Your high school encouraged everyone to go to college. The teachers you had always went above and beyond. Your grades were great and colleges were knocking at your door. You were the one that went on college visits, got great test scores, and landed the scholarship(s).

It could be any of these things or something else for many of you. But, regardless of what the circumstances may have been, all of you are now college graduates. NOW what? I don't know if you just finished 2,

...for the College Grad

3, 4, 5, or 6 years of college but, I do know this – NOW is a lot different than then. While you were in college, you experienced and accomplished several things.

Someone had a goal of getting into their first choice school and they got in. Someone wanted to get and maintain a perfect grade point average and they did that. Maybe you wanted to fall in love and you did. They said you needed an internship and you got 3 (overachiever...LOL). You joined every club, group, and organization that you could. You partied like never before, made friendships that will last forever, and graduated with honors.

Or, maybe you struggled in your classes. Maybe you are the one that did 4 years in 5 years. Some of you didn't reach the goals you set for grades and internships abroad. You came up short on several things but, you never gave up. You may have changed your major 5 times and are still not sure if you picked the right one. But, you still managed to get that degree.

I have 2 things to say to each group I just described – WHATEVER AND WHO CARES! Those days have NOW come and gone and NOW you are in the future that you planned for and there are other pressing issues at hand. There is no more quad, oval, or student union. Your lecture hall days are over. There are no more professors and office hours. You just paid somewhere between $9,000 to $40,000 per year more or less for your education through a combination of grants, loans, scholarships, and work study. But, you graduated and NOW have an average of $27,000 in

My Now...

student loan debt and in about 6 months you have to start paying that back...WTH! I know that's what you want to say or worse.

The reality of NOW is that you have some decisions to make. Do you already have a job or job offer? If so, that is great - 25% of college graduates do. But, if you don't, NOW what? Do you get an apartment with friends or move back in with mom and dad? 85% of graduates do the latter. What is your plan NOW – now that NOW has arrived? What seemed to be light years away is already here and some of you find yourselves not prepared for what you were preparing for.

NOW is defined as this present moment. The moment that we live in, in my opinion, is the most crucial time in our lives. But, our minds are so filled with regrets and successes of the past and fears and anticipations of the future that we cannot fully focus or benefit from the potential of today. So, the question is this - How are you going to make the most of the NOW moments that are going on in your life right NOW?

One of the best ways to do this is to understand that this is not the time to reminisce, recall, or ruminate your college days. You'll have plenty of time for that later. NOW is the time to get busy all over again. The world is a different place than it was when you started your college journey. You are a different person than when you started college as well.

You have been living in a bubble for the last few years. As a college student you have been isolated from the "real" world. Room and board were provided, food was everywhere, gyms were free, and living was easy. But, all of that is a memory. You are like Gill from Finding Nemo.

...for the College Grad

You have been working and working to get out and NOW that you are out – you find yourself floating in a plastic bag asking – NOW what. GREAT question!

NOW moving back in with your parents, if that is an option, is a valid option but, not a permanent option. NOW, let's face it – you don't really want to go back and they don't want you to come back either. But, this is not about what anyone wants. This is about what is necessary to be successful NOW and unless you royally screwed up, your parents and family will accept you back. So, don't try to make this a long term fix. Get in, get out, and move on. They already converted your room and you can't expect them to convert it back. Fit in where you can get in and be thankful for a roof over your head. NOW is not the time to be ungrateful. NOW is the time to get some kind of job somewhere and contribute to the household even if they say don't. They said you don't have to but, they really meant OMG – really! So, let's start generating some income and helping out. This is going to help your self-esteem and they are going to treat you as an adult and not a child.

NOW stay away from all of the old things that you left behind when you shipped off to college, if you end up going back home. It sounds harsh but, it's true. They say that old habits die hard and you killed a few if not all of those while you were pursuing that degree. You can't expect to move forward if you are looking backwards. NOW requires that you focus on your future and not your past. I have seen it happen time and time again. People go back and get in the same old groove that they escaped and get trapped all over again. Don't let that happen to you. This is the reason why going back home to be with your parents and family can't be a long term event. You can make change and give back AFTER you become successful.

NOW, if you are repulsed by the idea of moving back home and feeling like a failure or you have a job already, get yourself a roommate or two. You should be used to living with other people by now – family and then college. This is another valid option especially if you are all employed. NOW is not the time to carry any freeloaders. Make sure that everyone is doing their fair share and contributing their fair share and not using their unfair share. This type of collaborative living can teach you a lot in terms of negotiation skills, budgeting, teamwork, problem solving, and communication skills. What better time than NOW to learn those skills for success. Keep in mind that this can't be that frat house kind of grunge living situation. You're trying to be successful NOW. If that can't happen – move back home with you family.

NOW your success will not be dependent on what you know – only. Your success will depend on who you know and how well you leverage the relationships you've built over the past several years. If you did what you were supposed to do and not just what you wanted to do, then, you have cultivated friendships and relationships that matter NOW. You should have viewed your professors, classmates, co-workers, and acquaintances as valuable contacts that you would need NOW. A lot of students miss this step and struggle after college is over while those who spent their time networking are on the fast track to their future. So, get out that contact list and let your fingers do the walking and your lips do the talking.

...for the *College Grad*

NOW save everything you can and spend as less as you can. If you have the ability to put some money aside...do it NOW. That lifestyle that you want is not an option NOW unless you landed that 6 figure paycheck and position the moment you took your graduation gown off. If you did, you are the lucky one and I want to know you – call me NOW. All kidding aside, your goal NOW is to put away as much as you can while you are working towards success. A good place to start is to save 10% of your income every time some money hits your hands. Increase it if you can. The more you can save the better for you. It's okay to dream about that new Bugatti but, if you can't afford it, get that Aveo and treat it like a Bugatti.

NOW, I know you want that steak and seafood and you deserve it. But, not NOW. NOW it may be time to get some Ramen noodles, Sardines, Tuna, Peanut Butter, and crackers. NOW is the time for sacrifice. I guarantee that if you would sacrifice NOW you will benefit later. It WILL pay off. The mistake a lot of people will make is doing and getting too much too soon. Take it slowly. Sometimes a fast climb results in falling quicker. The goal is to actually make it and not fake it.

NOW get dressed. It's time to look the part of a college graduate in pursuit of a career. I know you are used to wearing Toms, Birkenstocks, and flip flops. You are used to being comfortable when you go to class – sweats, hoodies, and college swag. But, NOW it's time to wear that on the weekend and after hours unless that is the dress code for the job you are seeking. Most employers are looking at your outside before they hear you say a word. I know you are smart but, smart doesn't get a

My Now...

chance to speak if your bare feet enter the room before you do. Am I saying stuffy? No. But, I am saying professional.

NOW make some plans. You had a great plan in place when you were deciding to attend college. That plan just ended at the conclusion of your final day in college. But, the end of college is not the end at all. It is just the beginning. It is the beginning of the next phase of your life and that next phase needs to be planned NOW.

NOW, the first step of that plan is to get somewhere alone and begin to think and then write out what you want your future NOW to be. No one can do this for you. For the last several years you have been surrounded by all that is college. You did a great job planning your past NOW. That is evident by the degree that NOW graces your wall. Use your NOW NOW to ensure that your future NOW ends up just as successful. That happens in solitude. The last thing you want to happen is that you make it successfully through your next phase only to end up in a plastic bag floating and not swimming. Plan and swim – NOW.

...for the *College Grad*

My Now...

Chelle Lynne

Chelle Lynne fills many roles in her life – devoted wife, nurturing mother, loving daughter and selfless public servant. A 25 year veteran of the Army, she has served in peace and conflict. She is no stranger to adversity – assaulted as a teen, the death of her daughter in 2003, and most recently the death of her husband in March 2013 – but she continues to move forward in her life with grace and strength, sharing a story of resiliency. Published author of "Forged By the Fire of Adversity," she firmly believes there are no coincidences in life. There are blessings in the burdens we face, if only we are willing to see them, and we can emerge from the fire stronger for what we have endured. You can learn more about Chelle's latest projects and current speaking engagements at www.chellelynne.com.

Follow her on Facebook @Chelle-Lynne_AuthorMotivatinnal-Speaker

...for the *College Grad*

Dealing Positively with Adversity

Chelle Lynne

As you prepare to leave college and venture out into the big, wide world to chart your path, you probably have a mixture of emotions – pride, excitement, anticipation, and maybe a bit of fear. That is natural. You are about to begin the rest of your life. As you navigate that road we call life, the road will not always be smooth. You are bound to hit a few pot holes along the way. We all face adversity in our lives. Some hit small bumps. Some hit big bumps. Some people face less, while others seem to have more. The question, as I once read, is this – Is life going to be the grindstone that polishes you or tears you down? I believe we have a choice in how we answer that question.

You might be wondering how I came to start writing and doing presentations on resiliency in the face of adversity. Well, you might say life brought me to this place. As a woman of faith, I say the Lord brought me to this place. If you read my biography, you read about some of the things I have faced and am facing in my life. I was abandoned at birth but adopted by a wonderful, loving family. I was sexually assaulted as a teenager by a neighborhood predator. My daughter passed away at the age of 3 in January 2003. I deployed to war in 2006, witnessing the worst of humanity for a year in the form of bombings and beheadings, and lost three good friends. And most recently, my husband passed away in March 2013 from a sudden heart attack. Yes, I have seen my share of adversity.

There are several analogies frequently used to describe the adversity we face in our lives, a couple of which use the image of fire. One such analogy involves the use of fire to forge steel into a sword. Another analogy uses the image of fire purifying gold to bring out its luster. I personally like the analogy of fire forging steel because purifying gold with fire talks about appearance, but forging steel with fire talks about substance.

In metal work, forging is the process of using fire to superheat steel so that it can be shaped. People often think of sword making when they think of this process. The metal is heated in the fire, then pounded into the desired length and thickness and then plunged into cold water. This process is repeated numerous times. While on the surface we might think of this process as destructive, the process of repeatedly heating, pounding and cooling actually makes the steel stronger while molding it into the shape desired by the sword maker.

No matter which analogy one might prefer for explaining the role adversity can play in our lives, one thing is clear. Adversity will always be there in some form or shape, but we can emerge from the fire stronger and more resilient in handling other challenges.

As I talk about dealing positively with adversity, I must first admit that I have not always handled adversity this way. My preferred method before was always denial and avoidance. For you see, I was always the

...for the College Grad

consummate planner. I had a plan for everything -- my five-year plan, my ten-year plan, my plan for the Summer. I felt I could control everything, but control is just an illusion we convince ourselves we can achieve. My realization of just how wrong I had been came nearly 13 years ago.

I was 20 weeks pregnant with my second child when a routine ultrasound revealed some problems. Suddenly nothing was in my control. More ultrasounds created more questions that couldn't be answered. All I could do was trust that the Lord would give me the child I was supposed to have. When my daughter was born, she had multiple birth defects and wasn't expected to live. She defied all odds and not only lived, but thrived. Yes, her life was challenging, but she had an incredible fighting spirit. And she had a smile that could light up a room. While everyone else seemed to focus on what she didn't have or couldn't do, we chose to love and support her and focus on what she could do. We committed ourselves to creating a positive environment that would allow her to be whatever she was capable of being. We would not allow her to be defined by her diagnosis. Our positive approach yielded positive outcomes. We took each day with her as a precious gift and treated it as if it was our last because we never knew when that would be true. When she died at the age of 3, we could look back with no regrets, knowing we had done everything within our power.

As you look to deal positively with whatever situation you are facing, one important key is to be mindful and present in the moment. Too often we ruin the present by worrying about the future or the past. Being mindful is about being fully present and fully aware, moment by moment, paying attention to each experience and each situation without resistance, without judgment, without analyzing and without reacting. Often we resist the reality we are facing and our new and unwelcome current situation, believing that being present in the moment will only bring us more pain. Consequently we resist even more, which can, in fact, actually deepen our pain. Being mindful brings calm at the moments we need it most.

Yes, I know it sounds simplistic, but just start with one moment, one event, or one activity at a time. Look for the positive and appreciate the moment you are in right now without looking forward or back. One way to practice being mindful is to do awareness exercises. Find a quiet place and a quiet time. Now, listen to and feel your heart beat, listen to and feel your breath as it comes into and out of your lungs. Feel your blood as it pumps through your body. Do not talk yourself through it. Just stay still in the moment and observe as if you are inside your body watching it function. Were you able to stay still, or did your mind drift off? Did you resist the stillness by fidgeting or looking at the clock? Or did something distract you? Just be aware of what happened and practice again from time to time. Make this exercise of awareness part of your routine. You can schedule it into your day, perhaps first thing in the morning or last thing before bed. If you train yourself to be present in the here and now through practice, eventually you will find that it happens automatically and you start feeling more grounded and calm.

I hope this mini exercise helps you to focus on the present rather than being distracted by the past or future when you are in the midst of a situation that is challenging you and your resiliency. This exercise and several mantras I have developed over the past 10 years years have helped me to realign my thinking when in difficult circumstances. Remember, we can't control everything that happens to us, but we can control how we react to it.

There are no coincidences in life

We love to interpret events to find a meaning or causality to the way things work in our world. We are very fond of words such as coincidence, chance, fate, luck, karma and destiny when discussing life events. None of these words are really adequate to describe the things that happen in our lives. I am a firm believer that there are no coincidences in life. There is a reason for everything that happens, even when we don't understand what it might be. Only one understands it all, for He is the only one who sees the entirety – what was, what is, and what will be. Events work together and are interrelated to weave the fabric of our lives. They bring about change. They cause individuals to cross paths who might not otherwise meet. If you think of events as purposeful rather than random, you'll have a better appreciation for all things that happen, good or bad.

Ask "What," not "Why"

One of the first things we do when adversity strikes is to ask the question, "Why?" Why did this happen? Why me? Why us? Why now? Why do I have to go through this? It is natural part of our human nature to ask these questions, but asking why often doesn't yield any answers.

It seems to merely put us in a downward spiral of negativity. While "Why?" may seem to be the natural first question to ask, we must quickly move past that, or we risk getting stuck in a cycle of negative thinking and negative action. Typically when we ask "Why," we end up looking down and hanging our heads. We focus inward on ourselves and can miss the bigger picture going on around us. And lastly, by asking "Why," we allow anger and doubt to cloud our thinking. The simple act of questioning plants the seeds that allow doubt to spring up, and from that, anger can grow.

Instead of asking "Why?" when faced with adversity, a better question to ask might be "What?". What is the purpose for what I am enduring? What am I to learn from this experience? What is it that I should change in my life? What can I do to help others in this situation? By asking these types of questions, we keep our focus where it needs to be, upward and outward. An outward rather than inward focus allows us to see the connections between events and people.

Our experiences are our story

Our experiences are our story in life, a story that is meant to be told. Crises and tragedies can mold us and shape us and perhaps provide newfound perspective on life, but we shouldn't allow them to define us. If we allow an event to define us, the event is the focus and remains such, to the point where it can become a crutch used throughout life. A better avenue is to let our strength of character define us both during and after adversity. It is that strength of character which can have a profound effect on others if you are willing to share your story.

...for the *College Grad*

I used to be surprised when I felt compelled to say something to someone, only to hear them tell me, "You don't know how much I needed to hear that." I'm not surprised anymore. I know that when I listen to the voice inside me about what to say, or when I go where I feel compelled to go, I find that I have incredible opportunities to touch the lives of others. Those opportunities also bring me incredible blessings and satisfaction.

Blessings in the burdens

No matter what you are facing in life, there is always good that can come out of negative situations, but you have to be willing to look for it. If you focus on the negative, all you will see is the negative. It takes conscious effort to look for positives, but there are blessings in our burdens. If you allow it, your mindset will determine your reality. Positive thought will bring about positive results because the body follows the brain.

If you are having trouble looking for the blessings in your burdens, try doing an attitude exercise. This type of exercise helps to build an attitude of gratitude as a reminder of the little things we often take for granted or forget. List the letters A to Z down the left side of a sheet of paper and use each letter as a prompt for something that you are grateful for in your life and/or of all the fun experiences/people/places that you enjoy/have enjoyed.

Example:

A – apples – I love granny smith apples

B – beach—I loved it when my family would go to the beach every summer

C – cats – I adore my 2 cats, especially when they rub up against me purring

….And so on, for every letter in the alphabet.

By making a conscious decision to look for positives instead of allowing yourself to be controlled by negatives, you are better able to navigate the bumps in the road of life. A positive attitude and spirit will help you build resiliency, emerging from difficult situations stronger and better able to face the next challenge. We all are the product of our experiences because those experiences shape us. I wouldn't be the person I am today if I hadn't gone through what I went through with my daughter. Embrace whatever situation you find yourself in. Own it and look for a positive outcome. Do not allow the circumstance to dominate you.

Wishing you all the best as you hit the road!

...for the College Grad

My Now...

Nysheva-Starr

Nysheva-Starr is an innovator, writer, designer, speaker, and performing artist. She is the CEO of I-Gaian, Inc, a company primarily aimed at fostering cumulative growth for African Americans. She is the founder, creator, and arranger of Safari Kwenye Nafsi: Journey to Self, the African American Right to Rites of Passage Experience, a comprehensive and progressive series of passages geared towards documenting age set journeys for Black Americans. She has written a series of books which will be published soon, highlighting the principles that make early development successful, especially as it relates to Blacks. As an innovator/designer, she recently patented a garment she made for yoga practitioners. She is also one of the featured authors of the books, *My Vision, My Plan, My NOW* and *My Now for the Entreprenuer*.

Follow her on twitter @nyshevastarr.

For more information on the passages, send an email to info@i-gaianinc.com and/or visit the website at www.i-gaiainc.com.

...for the College Grad

Dear Younger Sibling:

August 2013

Greatness begins the moment you decide that just being good ain't good enough.

****Nysheva-Starr***

When you make the decision that you want to be great, you can start to achieve greatness by *simply* revamping each experience, event, and/or encounter to mark it to a greater degree than it was before. This means that you raise the stakes on your life...with everything. Once your life achieves this echelon flow from the fact that you've elevated how you see and do everything; you will realize the most important thing 'being on the road to greatness' teaches you – It Ain't *only* About You. That's right, you read correctly! Greatness is about your place in the world. It is about how you use who you are to make the world better. Greatness is the way in which you, the individual, empowers the collective.

So, the first thing I want you to ask yourself is, *'Do I want to be good or do I want to be great?'*

...

My Now...

Did you know that when I graduated from college I thought I was the shit? You probably realized that from the 'I'm the Shit' message that was on my mortarboard during graduation. No one could tell me I wasn't great! Before I even crossed the stage, I had a job offer with a great company doing work in a field I didn't even study in college making a competitive salary instead of an entry-level one. I had friends and status and I was considering applying to graduate school to study something that was going to accelerate me acquiring the prestige and influence that I knew I was gaining – I just didn't know what *that* was yet. I lived in a lower high class area, I went out on the town often and I got cozy with the boys when I wanted to. I was the ideal college grad merging into the main-stream. I was *good*. It was *good*. Life was *good*. Until it wasn't...

I *made so many mistakes. I didn't know. No one told me. I wish someone had, so I could've done things differently.* So, I'm telling you so **you can** do things differently.

...

It started when I accepted the job with that high end company. After all, the company was expanding, so there was room for growth and they had offices internationally, so I was banking on a possible *business trip to Malaysia, Honduras or maybe even Nigeria coming up in my not too distant future. You know how you feel like a choice you made is gonna turn out good.* That was me, especially since I wasn't thinking about **becoming** great, as far as I was concerned, that was a byproduct of my favorable situation. There were just a few things I had to work

...for the College Grad

through. First of all, this was a big company and many times I found myself drained in droves of ideas and input. For some reason (*I'll tell you the exact reason later*), during those times, my mind zoned out while my body did its best at feigning interest. It seemed like someone always had something to share – my wife, my husband, my fiancé, my kids, my dog, my cat, my chinchilla, ahhh, blah, blah, blah. To the average person it seemed like congenial conversation, but, to me, the frivolous shit that entertained the masses exhausted me. By month 4, 'faking the funk' (*that's an old school term, Google or Bing it*) was too hard to keep up. My second issue was with the dress code. Before you ask, yes, I knew they had a dress code when I took the job; what I didn't know was how something as menial as 'what you wear' can affect your whole day, for as long as you're wearing that outfit and even when you take it off. For some people, business women especially, choosing what to wear was something they looked forward to each night. It was hard for me to keep up. I mean, I've never really had a problem with business attire, but, then again, I never had to wear it 5 times a week for a minimum of 8 hours a day. *Guess what I discovered?* I really dislike business clothes – the shoes, the skirts, the sometimes blazer, Argghhhh! I DON'T LIKE WEARING THAT STUFF, NO MATTER HOW WELL *(sorry for shouting, I'm having flashbacks of my toes being squished on the inside sides of the shoes)* it looks on me. It feels confining, like I'm only able to move within the physical limits of my clothes' perforation. The irritation with my irritants distracted me. I didn't have the cushion of finals, gossip, deadlines and parties to hide behind. The realities of life were staring at me as if it were asking me 'if I could take it.' I was staring back and wanted to shout, 'I don't know, maybe, but, I don't want to.' *I still wasn't thinking about greatness' journey, so, even my confidence waivered.* I retracted my thought—I had to make this job work. I assuaged my dismay by focusing harder. After all, I was a professional. I organized accounts. I made spreadsheets. I translated documents. I facilitated meetings. I did paperwork. I wrote reports. Nope, focusing didn't help. I was bored. I felt stuck. It was too mundane. I'd hide out in my office, take off those damn shoes, pull my blouse out of whatever bottom I was wearing and put my feet up and close my eyes. For brief moments, I'd feel like Al Bundy, sans the hands in the pants *(Wikipedia 'The Bundy's).* I'd stay there for as long as I could reasonably get away with without someone getting suspicious; then I'd resentfully emerge again. This job wasn't me. It didn't fit. The moments of hiding out in my office stopped being effective at providing me with a reprieve. The outdoors was beckoning me. I obliged. I'd be momentarily entranced. *I noticed much later on how much I loved being outside. You should think about that now! Is there anything about yourself that you feel is a part of you, but, you never really recognized it as openly as you should have?* My 15 minute breaks turned into 30 minute interludes. It was getting harder to muster up the bravado to go back inside. I hated the office more than I hated the clothes. But, not just my office, offices in general zapped me. My boss took notice. I was too cowardice to tell her I was unhappy. *Honestly, my pride wasn't prepared to let go of what I had gotten.* When the monotony deepened from an influx of work; while others were overtly excited at the company's potential in the coming months, I covertly, gave not a damn as I sought change in walking to different areas using different routes to buy any sort of clothes that were different from what I had to wear for work. It pacified me. *Remember that authentic kimono we gave Mom for her birthday, I found it during one of my walks away from the job.* Anyway, my boss approached me again – this time, more disapprovingly. She was displeased with my work. I didn't blame her. It was suffering. I was too. Again, in cowardice, I made something up, I told her I was applying to graduate schools and that I didn't have the funds to get into one of the more prestigious schools and that that was saddening me. *I was still factoring on how a graduate degree could increase my social sphere. I should've walked away then, but, I was caught up in getting **that** American Dream...*

"Is that all it is?' she said, smiling, seeming somewhat relieved. "Well, it just so happens,' she began, 'that, in light of our company's growth, we want to make sure our employees are expertly qualified, so we're launching an Employee Graduate Program with two excellent schools," she said smirking. "Of course, you'd have to commit to us for at least three years once you get your degree, but I'm sure that's not going to be a problem for you, since, you like it here," she finished. 'You **do** like it here, don't you?" she asked hesitantly, trying not to conceal her uncertain wonder, but, not being successful.

'Uh, yeah, yes, I do...I like it a lot,' I quickly lied, hoping that my haste in answering would conceal my deceit.

Then its final,' she said. She started to walk away before turning back around. "You know, she said, 'I've been watching you and though the quality of your work has diminished in the past few months, you have great potential – that's why I recommended you for the program." "Just

My Now...

fill out the application as soon as possible and leave it on my desk, we'll take care of the rest."

Shit! Shit, Shit, I remember thinking. *And I was feeling like shit too. That's not the response I was looking for. I was looking for a way out. As you can imagine, this was Not Good.*

Yet...if I did it, in two years I'd have a MASTER'S DEGREE *and* I'd be two thousand dollars away from ninety percent of a six figure salary **and** I'd be two years away from thirty. I acquiesced. That made me feel great. *No, not really. I felt ashamed at the celebrations in my honor. Now when I think about it, I feel like a fraud.*

Graduate school was actually the first time I could feel the effects of not having a background in the field. Even my (almost) eighteen months as an employee didn't give me the leverage I needed to 'stay up' with the other students. It was not fun. I felt like I was working three times as hard as everyone else. My social life dwindled almost immediately after I began and I was coming into work early and staying late to keep my work up to par. I didn't want to give my boss a reason to question her defense of me. I did not have a *good* life. It sucked! I grew mad. The lure of my future looming over me was losing its hold as pushing towards a degree just to relish in the verbal accolades from others didn't seem worth it, especially if the degree wasn't in something that I actually *wanted* to do. Twenty-five felt like forty-five, on my way to a crisis. I had reached the point where I was pushing forward so hard that I was falling backwards too. *You know what that means don't you? It meant that I was at a stand still...unintentionally.*

I needed to do something. I paused...intentionally.

> *Pausing is the thing that comes right before waiting and happens instead of stopping. Its purpose is to allow for clarity so that as you move forward, your time is not wasted, nor anyone else's. Pausing gives you time to assess whether what you're doing is aligned with what you're thinking and how you're feeling.*

And then...I quit school. I only completed half the degree. I waited to tell my boss, hoping that 'time' would alleviate some of the embarrassment. It didn't. Guilt prevailed in its place. I rehearsed what I was going to say and knocked on her door. She happily obliged. When I entered her office, there wasn't the usual two chairs facing each other blocked by a desk in between set-up. The two chairs were side by side on one side of the desk as if in preparation for a more intimate conversation. Why was it like that? Were we expecting someone else to join us? Was *this* for me? I suddenly felt panicked. For a moment, I got scared and *wanted to just leave and never come back* – I figured she'd get the 'memo.'

"Have a seat," she said, pointing to the chairs." She was smiling, so I relaxed and pardoned my mind for making me afraid.

"I don't think you like it here," she began.' I was startled inside and hoped it didn't show on the outside. She was right, I didn't like it, but, I didn't say so. Instead, I averted her eyes.

"Do you know why we hired you," she went on, after, apparently getting what she needed from my silence? "Think about it," she said.

My Now...

"Why would an employer disregard the fact that a **recent college grad** (she said that in slow motion) did not major in what their company specializes in?" she asked rhetorically. "It's not like we're sure you'd be a *good fit*," she went on. What we look for," she began, are 'The Cans':

1) Can you communicate effectively?
2) Can you problem solve?
3) Can you work well with others, even someone you dislike and/or disagree with?
4) Can you create?
5) Can you meet a deadline?
6) Can you ask for help?"
7) Can you seek out understanding where you're lacking?

"You see," she finished, "who cares what your major was if you can't do those things"...then, if you *Can*...theeenn, we assess if you fit. And you dear, do not fit.

Good Luck!

I shook her hand and left her office. We both knew I was not coming back. I was glad it ended cordially. When I received a letter from her three weeks after I left, I thought it was to see how I was doing. It was a bill for the tuition I owed the company. I smiled. It was all good. I imagined her smiling as she signed it. I was good. *I wonder if smiling made her enjoy her job more. Nah, it couldn't, cause I was smiling and I had no job.* I felt *great*. Life was getting good.

....

...for the College Grad

I still wanted to travel, so I did. I intentionally went from job to job to job. And I wasn't pausing or waiting or stopping. I was searching for 'where I fit.' It took me a few more years of wandering professionally to figure out the type of profession I needed to have to match with the type of person I am to bring out the type of employee I wanted to be. *Remember when I told Mom & Dad that 'I was going to a lot of different places – I really was, but, not the way they thought. They thought I was doing great things. I thought I was too, now I know I was.*

I got hired to work for a budding company doing various levels of interactive development. I didn't even know what that was, but, as it seemed, neither did they – they were discovering it as they were creating it. I was brought on as a collaborator. Even though this was not an artistic job, there was room to roam. The environment appeared more like an adult Montessori haven with a classroom feel, so, it didn't take long for me to feel like I was thriving. I asked lots of questions. I listened and was listened to. We debated contrasting concepts and tweaked and/or proposed better ones. Inconsistencies were queried freely and successes were rewarded loudly. I was also able and encouraged to sit alone and explore if I needed and/or wanted to. It seems that that fostered an intuitive and strategic side (for myself and my peers) and the bosses took notice. When, one day, exasperated over trying to defend a point to my work nemesis, my boss, with the wherewithal of a sage said, "Why don't you go outdoors for a bit and *feel* your way through it." Honestly, the first time he said that, I thought they were firing me. "It might help you," he urged me. I did and *it* did. I came back rejuvenated and ready. With a clearer, more focused mind, my thoughts were conveyed effortlessly. *He* smiled. I did too. Clearly, he (my boss) had made a *great* observation of me and followed through with an effective response. From then, my walks were encouraged; as long as my bosses knew, by any correspondence, that I was heading out and as long as my contribution upon return correlated with how much time I had been out. *I was so grateful for their trust in me, that I never abused it.* There was one time, I came back to the office after two hours and they thought I had quit. But, I was in the library creating contrasting presentations based on my dominantly visual learned colleagues versus my dominantly audibled learned colleagues. It went very well. I smiled so hard on that day, my jaw muscles ached. Everything seemed to have a point at this job, like, it all tied in. The managers had found a way to mesh the personal and professional worlds of their employees without zapping out on either. To top that off, you wore what was comfortable, as long as it was professional. *You know that was a hit for me – right?* Instead of getting lost in the freedom of autonomy and self discernment and judgment, 'me' was found.

By the time my six months probationary learning curve passed, tenacity and integrity were the default products of my work ethic. The results were favorable. I smiled.

I was smiling all the time. It seemed my first boss' secret had been exposed; that smiling was an involuntary response to a life that was being enjoyed. Sibling...are you smiling?

He scheduled a meeting – just between him and I. "I've evaluated your progress over the last few months and as your probation is terminating, I'd like to see how you're doing," the director was saying to

...for the *College Grad*

me. "It's goo...," I started to say, "it's great," I decided on after. I was calm. "It seems so," he said, unable to hide his glee. "You're doing an incredible job," he said, "and I would love to have you as part of the team for as long as you like – you just fit," he finished. "I'd like that," I replied with a chuckle. "There's just one thing," he asked, with a tad bit of concern. "You smile a lot, like just now, is that genuine or is it a developed defense mechanism, he asked, "don't worry, your job is secured, "it helps us to know stuff like this about our staff to better support them." *I started to speak, I stopped. He waited. I started again. I paused.* "It's because I've learnt how valuable fun is to overall success and when I smile, its an involuntary affirmation that confirms that I'm enjoying what I'm doing." He pondered a bit, in slight accedence. Silence presumed, but, not the awkward kind, and then unconsciously, in unison, we both smiled.

I thanked him and left the office. I was coming back. My job was *great*. Life was *great*. I had become *great*.

...

Soon after, thirty came. I got together with former friends and noticed that not too many of them seemed genuinely happy. *We don't hang out nearly enough to still be considered friends.* Their false bravado almost successfully hides their seething emptiness, an illusively grandiose affair to watch, I must say. Loathed conversation filled the air. I could tell they were wondering about me. I wasn't saying much – *just simply smiling.* I was happy. I excused myself for air on the patio when the rambunctiousness of comparisons became too much to bare. I was there

My Now...

for a bit when I heard my former social BFF saying most cockily, "Well, I got my American Dream, I'm a -. "I got it," I unintentionally mumbled audibly, "of course," I continued, unfazed by the looks of concern. And then I started smirking. *They glanced at me from their seats, about 200 feet away.* "As I was saying, my former BFF said, trying to recover her thoughts unabashedly, but, I started laughing. Hard. It was unintentional too, but, I didn't want to pause and waiting seemed futile. It was a forceful laugh - a flowing, epiphanous cacophony. *They were staring now.* I teared. It felt *Great.* "What's funny," she asked annoyed?

> "There is no such thing as the American Dream," I began from out on the patio. That is a faux. There are as many dreams as there are dreamers" I went on, intentionally, making my way back into the communal space. And since the number of Americans is so vast, could it also be that getting to **your version of the American Dream** is varied too? Isn't that really what success is, I asked her, pointedly (but rhetorically)? "Yes, but," she attempted to answer (She didn't get or care that it was rhetorical) "I'm not done," I said, curtly. 'The American Dream' is about the character of the person making the choices." It's about approaching fear time and time again until you beat it. And it's about doing things for yourself, not 'cause everyone else is doing it."

It was time for me to go. I had stayed two hours pass my intended time and had said ten minutes more than what was expected and was two seconds away from being out the door when she came up to me, "That was *great*," she said. "You look well," she said. "I feel well," I said, "I am well." I exited...smiling and *grate*ful.

...for the College Grad

POST SCRIPT

College grads are messengers. They are vessels for change and in many regards, they spearhead that change. Do not take that responsibility lightly. It is not enough to only speak out against what's wrong with the world; you, being more socially, intellectually, and emotionally prepared to handle more of the grievances posed to the world are required to administer efforts towards changing it. Did you know that, on graduation day, when you reach out to shake the hand of whomever that you're actually honoring your end of the silent pact that says: 'Yes, yes, I'm ready – I'm ready to become great.' And then they give you that *superfluous* paper...

I came up with a list of rules that you can benefit from, to help you be smarter with choosing your career. Please make less mistakes than I did!

My Now...

> ## The Meter towards Greatness
>
> *Rule #1: Be true to yourself and others. Withholding important thoughts and feelings creates misery for all sides.*
>
> *Rule #2: Discover what you're passionate about and why and then do something about that - you're passionate about it for a reason.*
>
> *Rule #3: Know what type of person you are in a work environment, knowing that you're an introvert might deter you from working for a large company (I told you I'd come back to it later)*
>
> *Rule #4: Assess whether you need to be in a creative environment to flourish?*
>
> *Rule #5: Think about the setting: indoors, outdoors, combination thereof and/or whether you prefer a somewhat set environment versus an ever changing one.*
>
> *Rule #6: Yes, it is important to be comfortable with the dress code. Do you mind uniforms? Can you do casual every day? Are business clothes your thing?*
>
> *Rule #7: Knowing another language can only enhance your overall human experience.*
>
> *Rule #8: While on the job, do not punish yourself with an embellished or false reality of your knowledge or will.*

    P.P.S. Sorry for this letter being so long, I wanted to make sure I covered everything. Anyway, come over so we can watch a movie together. It'll be great to see you. I'll bring the popcorn, you can bring some drinks. I miss you. By the way, CONGRATULATIONS.

                                                With love,
                                                Your Older Sibling

...for the *College Grad*

My Now...

Rodney Burris

Educator, National Speaker, Youth and Family Advocate, and Entrepreneur; these are some of the words used to describe Rodney Burris. In addition to a wide range of career experience, the common thread among all his ventures is a strong desire to strengthen communities.

Mr. Burris holds a BA in Psychology from the Johns Hopkins University and an MS in Management of Nonprofit Agencies from Capella University. He is deeply rooted in neighborhood empowerment and has tutored struggling students, encouraged area leaders to become more involved in the community, and reconnected fathers with their children, advising them on parenting and life skills. Rodney is also an avid promoter of business development and entrepreneurship. His combined knowledge of non-profit experience and business-startup has been used to assist scores of interested learners. He is also one of the featured authors of the book, My Vision, My Plan, My NOW!

RodneyBurris@mail.com
www.RodneyBurris.com
@RodneyCBurris

...for the College Grad

Not Another J.O.B.!

Rodney Burris

"I'm just trying to get a job." We've all heard this statement before. In fact, many of us have uttered these very words out of our own mouths. And we think we mean every bit of it. But many of us don't know the detriment behind these words, and the cycle of unfulfillment they can lead us in. You see, we say this when we get to the point of exhaustion with our present options. It's more an expression of unhappiness or dissatisfaction, than a statement of fact. When we say, "I just a want a 'job', what we really mean is, "I just want my builds paid", or "I am just trying to get enough to accomplish this/that goal", ...or, quite often, what we really mean is, "I just want to be happy".

And herein lies the problem. If we don't know our reason for work, we will continue to be unhappy. We will continue to feel undervalued, or under-achieving. We don't just want to work another J.O.B.; instead, what we really want, is to find that sense of self that comes with operating in our Career. This chapter will help us define and find our chosen Career, by teasing out the differences between the two, and setting us on a path of self-discovery and self-fulfillment that will ultimately land in the Career of our choosing.

My Now...

Let's begin.

Tip #1: Don't just work a job, find a career

There is an old adage that says, "Do what you love, and you'll love what you do." It is also common to hear, "money can't buy happiness." Money is best perceived as the byproduct of your work, not the Product. When Bill Gates started off making the windows operating system in the late 80's, his vision was to make the personal user experience with a computer, easier. His goal wasn't to become a billionaire. When Mark Zuckerburg created his social media network back in college, it was for the desire to help people connect, first all over his campus, and then all over other college campuses. Dollars came as a byproduct of them working their goal. They were passionate about it, and were persistent.

The first step is enjoying your work. Your career may make a lot of money for you, or your career may not equal a lot of money for you. Either way, you must start from a place of Passion, and Persistence. Mother Theresa, for example, worked in her career; it was her persistent passion. The same could be said for Mahatma Gandhi, as well as for a little shop owner not too far from your home who, working for 30 years, never became a millionaire, but who knew more about his product than anyone you know. They all did what they loved; they ended up Loving what they did. You must start from a place of Passion, and let money be a byproduct. If not, you'll end up chasing dollars, and losing sight on your happiness and sense of self.

Tip #2: Know the Differences between a Job and a Career

"Alright, so how do I know if I have a job or if I'm in my career?" -- Good question. Each has some clearly identifiable attributes. Let's list them here. We'll start with a Career:

A career is something that

- You are proud of, you feel good when you do it
- You love to do; you have a certain energy about it. It doesn't feel like 'work' to you
- You have opportunity for growth; you clearly see advancement: better/different/more for yourself, and of your impact
- Makes you a decent amount of income; for your needs, for your plans, for your trajectory
- Defines your personality well, you self-identify with it. It simply feels, natural
- The benefits are great; More than just health/dental/vision, you get things out of this that money can't buy, or that are intangible, or that would simply cost too much (money/time/effort) to get these same things elsewhere
- [What else? What would you like your career to bring to you? -- Feel free, write down some ideas at the end of this chapter; use this book as a reference point for those goals.]

Whenever you are gainfully engaged in activities that promote the attributes above, you my friend, are moving further along into your career. You are becoming who you ideal yourself to be. You are self-actualizing; i.e., the active process of working on yourself, so that you achieve the fullness of what you hope/believe your potential to be.

There are some key terms to remember here: 'process', which means it's not necessarily instant, and, 'active', which means you are constant & diligent in your efforts while in this process. Both Kobe Bryant and Michael Jordan have legendary rumors about how much they practiced: before games, after games, during the season, offseason, with the team, alone, using personal trainers, etc. And that sort of 'active process' works for any field, not just sports. For example, computer gurus Bill Gates & Steve Jobs each spent about 10,000 hours during their teenage years practicing software skills. These produced for us the Microsoft and the iPhone/Pad/Pod/Mac technologies, respectively. Being active in your process is giving it intentional focus as work to get it done.

So, that helps us get a grasp on what we should be looking for in a Career, but what about for a Job? From now on, when you think of a J-O-B, I want you to think of something that keeps you

Just

Over

Broke

Think about it. You have worked part-time jobs before. You have worked full time jobs before. You know what it's like to get paid by the hour. And you know what it's like to miss a few hours each week, and the resulting impact it has on your paycheck. -- You remember vividly what it's like to earn a paycheck that gives us just enough money to eat, just enough to keep your phone on, and just enough to get back in forth to

...for the College Grad

work. You may have had a dollar to throw on an extra bill or two. But after all of that, how much were we really have left with? We weren't broke, but we were 'just over' it.

Let's keep in mind; broke doesn't always have to mean money. I'll explain that in second. First, let's delve a little deeper into the definition of 'job'. Let's suppose a J.O.B. is also the antithesis of Career, in every sense of the word; meaning, whatever a Career is, a JOB is not.

With that new definition, a JOB can be described as the following:

1) Does not make you happy, it makes you miserable
2) You may not necessarily be proud of it -- instead, it may be something that was expected of you, or it could have been an opportunity that you would have felt bad in the eyes of others had you turned it down
3) You may not necessarily love to do it -- Let's be clear on this, all things being taken care of, a Career is something that you would do, for Free. You Love to do it. In fact, it doesn't even feel like 'work'. If your occupation doesn't naturally produce this inspiration, it is a job.
4) You may not have/feel/perceive the opportunity for growth. -- Raises, eventually, will happen. Promotions, after some period, are going to come. But if you don't feel like you are getting better, as a person; that is, if you don't feel that the quality of your emotional/personal/psychological state of being is improving because of what you do, then you are not doing something that lends itself to life/vitality, *For You*--someone else

maybe perfectly fine in that same environment, but for you it is hazardous; it is not a life-giving environment for you. A fish, for example, thrives in the water. So does a dolphin. So does a seahorse. Take either of those creatures, throw them in the lush, fertile warm environment of a rain forest, and watch how well they thrive. Despite all of the life that is teaming through the rainforest, each of those creatures would die quickly in that environment. --The Point: Opportunity to grow has everything to do with you, and very little to do with the actual job. Others could do very well in a place that you are squandering in. Vice versa, you may feel within yourself the opportunity to thrive, where others see only struggle, strife, and strain. Don't base this opportunity on others. You have to look within yourself, and be truthful with what you find there.

5) For a job, the money doesn't seem to go as far it used to, to make you *'feel better'* about where you are and what you are doing -- I had a buddy of mine who used to make a respectable amount of money working in a firm in New York. The economy hit a recession, and he was laid off. He found himself working a very demanding job the following year, with great pay. But he was miserable, and he didn't feel he had a life outside of work. He ended up staying on that job for less than a year before he pushed to find an opportunity where the money (pay), was not his only source of solace for the occupation. He needed to feel connected to it. Money was important, but not worth his stagnant unhappiness.

6) A j.o.b. does not seem to fit your personality well; it's hard for you to personally identify yourself with it -- Often we get confused and stay longer with a particular opportunity because 'we are good at it'. Not because we love it. Not because it fulfills us. Not even because it is a step towards something we really want to do. We are just doing it, because we don't really have something else to do instead. I have another friend who constantly communicates to me that just because he does something well, doesn't mean he enjoys doing it. This particular guy is very disciplined, very detail oriented, very dedicated to see a task through to its completion. Because of these traits, he was naturally good at maintaining the financial books of a business (the accounting) and reporting it at yearend to the proper authorities. But he detested that work. For him, it felt like dead-end, monotonous scrutiny of data that he wished he didn't have to think about. So he sought hard to find someone to replace those duties while he focused on what he felt his true gift was: innovative quality-control and process-management. For some, the opportunity to be an accountant represents a fulfilling Career. For him, although skilled at it, he did not self-identify as an accountant.

With all its wonderful attributes and positive possibilities, a Career can be great. Working a JOB, however, can be a depressing and self-defeating undertaking, as it represents absence of all the qualities associated with a career.

My Now…

At this point, we can gain new insights into the acronym, "Just Over Broke." As I said earlier, being broke can be much more than not having money. In fact, you have can have money, and still be broke. How so?

The definition of broke is *the state of not having any liquid cash to move, to spend, or to give to others*. As such, you could be considered *broke* in many different ways. For example, you can be so emotionally spent from working a job that you just don't have any more love/joy/happiness to give to their family when they get home. You can also be socially spent; nonprofits and human service workers often call this 'burnout'. You can feel personally spent; i.e., your sense of self simply does not match (or worse, is at odds) with your current occupation. You can feel physically spent; tired, sick, worn-down from not having rested properly, or because your work environment is physically exhausting (too hot, too cold, too many flights of stairs, too many germs, too much asbestos, etc.). Not having any more of any of these currencies to give, to move around, to spend, means that you are 'broke', in that regard. -- The interesting thing, you could have all your bills paid with some money left over, and still be broke in one of these areas. Working in your Career, these areas get replenished regularly. Working a Job, and these areas often hover around *just over broke*.

In conclusion, it is not our desire to be unhappy; or to live in a state of unfulfillment; or to be overly-stressed; or under-rewarded for our efforts. We all would like to get to the place where we feel assured that we are properly compensated for the work that we put in. As a college grad, you now have one of the basic tools required in our society to move into healthy, mutually beneficial period of employment -- you can now move into your Career.

Conversely, you can choose to simply do what so many of us have done, which is not properly apply ourselves to learning the true nature of our career (i.e., what makes us happy, what gives us life, how we best fit in with the world around us). Instead, many of us just simply 'go to work'; we a find a J.O.B., and we stick there -- miserable or not. Unfortunately, we find ourselves 'just over broke' financially (or emotionally, or physically, or socially, or etc.) when we work these kinds of opportunities. They are not opportunities that lend us life, not opportunities we love, and not opportunities we are necessarily proud of.

Because of all of this, we should do our due diligence to place ourselves in a place that we are proud of, that we do love, and which Gives us Life. We should enter into our Career. This chapter helps you begin to assess the tools of self-discovery, so that you can properly move in this regard.

I wish you God's Speed.

My Now...

Chris Wilchcombe

Chris Wilchcombe was made in Detroit and is Chairman and CEO of Bob Works Inc. Where We Make the Tool Maker's Life a Little Easier and Where we Only Do What Works!

...for the College Grad

So You Finished... Now What?

Chris Wilchcombe

Humility B4 Honor
Humility is fair but life is au contraire
We bear the stares and dare to be
different, some leave a scent that says
hello dear My name is fear for those
that stay near the rear.

We're not lost in space we can trace each failure's
face, because we kept the pace intertwined
strength laced, glowing face on that onward
pace, weary but not broken slow but steady
always prepared to be, what in our minds
we were designed to be.

Humility is simplicity that lays the ground for the sound
kept in our chest when we believe we are better
than the rest. B4 Honor Humility must test to see
How good are the best cause we have an obligation to the rest.

So we should welcome the Test.

By C. Wilchcombe

Okay college graduate − You finished! Great accomplishment! Congratulations − So happy for you! NOW, life starts.

My Now...

At the end of every episode of the cartoon G. I. Joe, tips were given and then he would say, "Knowing is half the battle." Well, I have some "knowing" for your battle!

Here's the real truth – Your NOW actually started when you STARTED college. But you bought into the idea that you had to wait four years before you launched your career. Maybe you looked for an internship but you couldn't get one. But you didn't worry because you were making good grades and getting READY for your career to launch AFTER you get that magical piece of paper. But the reality is, if you didn't begin your career while you were garnering your education, you are way behind. Did you actually believe that employers were lined up at the door waiting to give you a job after graduation? Let's take a look at the real world.

You've all heard the wonderful statistic that college graduates will make between two to three million dollars over a lifetime. Sounds pretty good, right? What you might not realize is that it is difficult to graduate with a liberal arts degree and start making $50K. Even if you get your master's degree, when you begin working in the United States, you are most likely going to be single and will be paying up to 33% or more in income taxes. When you take a look at that first pay stub, you just might find yourself truly shocked at how little you will be actually taking home to pay the mortgage, car notes, utilities, food, insurance, credit cards, and let's not forget the amazing student loan bill that appears six months after graduation!! Soon you realize that a job truly means J. O. B. – <u>J</u>ust <u>O</u>ver <u>B</u>roke! Welcome to the American Dream.

The sad reality is that for a good majority of people, the so-called American Dream is a recurring nightmare. An August 2013 Gallup Poll found that nearly 27% of workers 18 to 29 were under-employed IF they had a full-time job. Even if you land a good, full-time job, most are not working in their major field. Many more are only able to find part-time work after they get their diploma and have to live at home with their parents. Most of my peers that I currently have contact with are sick and tired of what they are doing. They never really wanted to do what they are doing but they got themselves a job because they felt that was the right thing to do. They have missed their particular calling primarily because they don't know what that calling is!

What most people don't understand is that education is a huge, billion dollar industry. It is a game of numbers that the industry is desperately trying to keep going – often at the expense of the students they are supposed to be serving. From the beginning you are taught that great grades equal success in life. What they DON'T tell you was that A students train B students to work for C students because nine times out of ten the person who runs your company isn't necessarily an A student and they just hire A students and B students to work for them.

If only you had been told that you could have gotten a GED and a trade at a two year school and then finished up the last two years in a four-year program without having to pay thousands and thousands of dollars. It would have been a terrific way to avoid the bondage of student loans! What if you started a business when you started college then you would have created an extra income or outlet for yourself. More importantly, most students in college are never taught any aspect

My Now...

of financial literacy. Ironically, even some accountants don't know how to handle money; they know how to handle other people's money. One thing you should definitely start to focus on is how you want to retire if retirement is in your book, and how do you possibly expect to earn a living and put money away if that is what you want to do.

If you don't want to end up working in the 40 to 60 year ponzi scheme of Social Security, you need to take some advice from G. I. Joe. – KNOW! Now that you are out of college, learn about REAL life. Find out as much as you can about business and finance. Get to know the many other options out there. I suggest that you read very widely on financial literacy and how to take control on the little money that you are earning. Move out of the realm of the J. O. B. worker into the realm of the true American Dream.

The bottom line is, you went and spent a lot of money to go the school – now you really have to get a job to pay that money back. Even if you don't owe a lot of money, you still have to see what kinds of opportunities are available. As the classic saying goes, "Don't hate the players, hate the game." If you want to be truly successful, here are a few basic steps to get started:

Get a journal. Write down your goals. Actualizing your goals makes you much more likely to reach them. Don't just write it once and put it away. Keep looking at it. Remind yourself why you are sacrificing now.

Start plotting a short term plan and how you are going to get there. And listen to me very carefully – it is **not** going to be by you working, because work is designed for you not to Ever get enough time to do things for yourself or your family. The system is designed for a huge labor force and they always want you to be a laborer.

Whatever your craft is, you must have a global NOW perspective. Success is not just going to be within the borders of the United States. Frankly, that is not where your competition lies. I do not believe that most students are adequately prepared for global society in a four-year program or most collegiate programs. But you need to educate yourself in the local library or books online, or find books for free to find out what this global market is about and how you can leverage your degree in a global market. Go to the library because most of these resources are free. Pick up material that will help you in sales, help you in negotiations, and help you in being able to close a deal. These are the individuals who are most sought after.

If you don't decide to start your own business, you are going to have to be very well equipped for the job market. You are going to have to stand out. You have to be better than everyone else. You are going to have to be smarter that everyone else if you want to maintain a job. Maintaining a job is almost an oxymoron because there is no maintaining a job when the bottom line is that there are very few companies in this world that will retain you once the bottom line is changed. Make yourself indispensable.

Be indispensable. You have an opportunity to be the consumer or the producer. Be the producer. The producer provides for the consumer. If you can put yourself in that type of situation and deliver, you will never be out of work. You will always be looked at as the one who can get the job done. A lot of people claim they can get the job done. A lot of people think they can get the job done. There are very few people who **can** get the job done.

In life there are risks and rewards. No one is telling you to be a gambler but, frankly, playing it safe has never yielded tremendous rewards. You may risk and fail at every point! You will never know if you don't try. Risk and reward go hand in hand. High risks almost always yields high rewards. Low risks almost always yield low rewards. You have to find out what you are made of. You have to find out what kind of mettle you have to execute the plan for your life. I can tell you to do X. I can tell you to do Y. I can give you the steps to plan it out, but your plan is for you. I can give you some pointers, utilize what you can utilize.

I am telling you what I had to do in order to truly educate myself to make progress in life. It's been 20+ years of praying, self studying, listening, and making mistakes. I actually didn't think about it. Like some of you, I wanted to be a doctor, lawyer or maybe even a congressmen writing laws. But things changed for me and I fell into my sweet spot. And you WANT to fall into your sweet spot and what works for you. Nothing worth having in life is easy.

Life has its sweet spots and treachery. Life has its downward spirals and life has amazing moments. You will have to choose what's going to be best for you. The hard part is that it may not be walking in your family's footsteps. Now if your family has already created a system for you, I would take hold of that system to see if I can merge it or morph it into something great versus not doing anything with the particular system that has already been set up by the sweat of their brow. Don't be afraid to utilize the advantage of a good family system.

Another important tip is to have several streams of income, if possible. A contingency plan is so very important. What happens to you when you get sick? What happens when your company downsizes and you are out of a job? What happens if your credit is less than perfect? What if you have a single income family? How will your family survive if something serious happens to you? If you don't foresee the contingencies of life when you are young, you could make some serious mistakes. Be prepared.

Once you find your successes and failures in life, it is your responsibility to pass on your knowledge and experience to the next generations. Remind them that a degree has its limitations in the real world.

What sets you apart from those other 6000 applicants? Your grades? Well 3500 of them had straight A's. What is going to separate you from being the person most sought after and most desirable? It's not going to be your resume. It's not going to be how well you are dressed. It's not going to be any of the above. It's going to be what's between your two ears and what your mouth can project, and what kind of persona you bring to the table and whether you can you deliver. People will hire an under-degreed individual before they hire a several degreed individual if the person can close the deal, sell the product, and get it done. Pass the knowledge on to everyone.

So again, congratulations on your degree. Congratulations on the things you've accomplished. But now the real world comes into view. What are you prepared to do? And what are you prepared for? That is what you need to be asking yourself. Another degree may not do what you are looking for. Another degree is not going to put you in a position to where you are indispensable because just like you got an MBA someone else can get an MBA. And there is always going to be someone who can get better grades than you. And there is always going to be someone who is better at what you do, but they are not necessarily indispensable. People know who the real leaders are and who the indispensable people are--Be One! Don't Try, Your Time is NOW....DO IT OR GO HOME!!!!

...for the College Grad

My Now...

Adebayo O. Adegun

Adebayo O. Adegun a.k.a. Make My 'Mpact holds a Bachelors' Degree in Technology (Electrical/Electronics), Masters' Degree in ICT, and a Diploma in Educational Psychology. He has about 19 certifications in IT and Management with 12years experience. Some of his areas of expertise are Management of IT Services, IT Trainings, IT Projects, IT Marketing, Deployment of Google Apps and Business Intelligence Solutions, Creativity, Team Building, Critical Thinking, Strategic Planning, and Personal Leadership. Adebayo is a Motivational Speaker, Career Counsellor & Visionary Thinker.

He had a distinctive career as a System Administrator/Trainer, System/Network Administrator/Facilitator, Server/Security Administrator/Facilitator, and Technical/Training Manager/Team Lead with A2J, International Data Management, NIIT and LearningMinds respectively. He was an IT Consultant to some banks, telecommunication, pharmaceutical and manufacturing firms, private and public educational institutions.

Adebayo is the Founder and President at CrossTie Solutions Limited, an organization aimed at improving Productivity and Professionalism of individuals and businesses.

www.crosstiesolutionsltd.com
crosstiesolutionsltd@gmail.com
www.facebook.com/CrossTieSolutionsLimited

...for the *College Grad*

A Knot Between the Educational Sector and Living a Meaningful Life

Adebayo O. Adegun

Allow me to start this chapter by sharing this excerpt by Jeff Selingo on "Congratulations, College Grad. Now Tell Us: What Did You Learn"

"It's college commencement season. Across the country, moms and dads, grandparents, and other family members are gathering on campus quads, football fields, and in basketball arenas to celebrate a rite of passage for the Class of 2013.

The graduates are now ready for the next stage of their life—a job (hopefully), their parents' basement (maybe), graduate school, law school, or maybe the Peace Corps or Teach for America. They're definitely older than when they went off to college. They're probably heavier. And with a bit of luck, they're more mature than when they left high school.

But did these graduates actually learn anything in college to deserve that diploma?

There's much debate these days about the return on investment of a college education. Much of that conversation is focused on what students spend on college compared to what they get in return in terms of a salary. But if the purpose of college is to get an education, why don't we measure the return on investment in terms of what students learn in college? After all, it's the learning that we're actually paying for when we write tuition checks, not training for a job that might be obsolete in two years.

Here's the problem: we don't know for sure how much students learn in college. As much as we spend on college, no bottom-line evaluation method exists for measuring what actually happens in the classroom and how that eventually translates into the value of the degree. Sure, there are the U.S. News & World Report rankings, but they mostly measure the students on their way in the door (how many students a college rejected, SAT scores) or how much colleges spend on faculty or students.

As much as colleges say they dislike the U.S. News rankings, they prefer them to any alternative that might try to rank colleges on how much students learn. Many colleges would like to keep prospective students and parents in the dark when it comes to how much value they end up adding to a student's life.

The main reason for this, the researchers found, was a lack of rigor. Through surveys they learned that students spent about 12 hours a week studying on average, much of that time in groups. Most didn't take *courses that required them to read more than 40 pages a week or write more than 20 pages over the course of an entire semester.*

Students who studied alone did better, as did students whose teachers had high expectations or assigned a significant amount of reading or writing. Those who majored in the humanities, social sciences, hard sciences, and math did the best. And the majors that did the worst? Education, social work, and the most popular major on US college campuses: business.

To determine how these students fared after college, the authors later resurveyed more than nine hundred of them after graduation. Not surprisingly, the students who scored the lowest on the also struggled in life after college. They were three times more likely than those scoring at the top to be unemployed, twice as likely to be living at home with parents, more likely to have run up credit card bills, and less likely to read the news or discuss politics.

Now, many students graduating this month might think its fine that they skated through college. But for students and parents who paid the tuition bills thinking they were getting a rigorous and life-changing experience, they deserved better. So do potential employers who will hire this month's graduates. We need more authoritative and accurate ways of measuring the value that a college adds to a student's life than some arbitrary rankings system created by a magazine that doesn't even publish anymore."

THE MEANING YOU CRAVE

The educational sector is the fabric of the general society saddled with the responsibility of grooming and equipping us with formal and non-formal education in the form of knowledge, skills and training; skills which may not be initially possessed or which may need polishing. You must understand that this may not necessarily be on paper like we've been made to believe that the day we don't go to school with our bags, we're very likely going to play.

> *Learning can take place anywhere, anytime, even without pen and paper!*

CAREER CONCERNS OF STUDENTS

Many students around the world believe for one to be successful in life, one must go through the conventional primary, secondary and tertiary institutions. But this belief is seldom their fault as many parents have turned themselves to 'Brain Programmers'. They made us all follow this pattern invented by yet to be identified philosophers. Anyone could go through any primary and secondary school, but when it comes to tertiary school, fundamental choices have to be made BY us not FOR us! Many a student is burdened with the choice of the right course to study or is not conversant with the challenges of the outside world. We have been made to believe by society that a college certificate will automatically translate to a job in the labor market. But Alas! That is a farce. College only equips you with basic skills necessary to forge ahead in the ever-changing world of work. So, how does one adapt to these changes?

> *Change has always been the only constant thing that is.*

Anxiety is one sure thing you'd feel upon graduation, but it's natural to feel that way. That uncertainty won't go away quickly as it is part of our lives. We all wake up with several expectations, many of which remain oblivious. Now is the time to learn that career management is not a terminal process but a lifelong pursuit.

YOUR DREAM JOB

Be not deceived, a ripe fruit catches every bird's fancy. Many people look where you look, crave what you crave, search the key words you search, apply where you apply and want the opening in the multinational company that you also want. Honestly, for anything desirable in life there is competition. Can you beat this competition? Yes! You can. All you need do is just build a comparative advantage. And what precisely is this advantage? It is comprised of three key things:

A – Assets

A – Aspirations

M – Market Realities

Your assets could be SOFT or HARD.

Soft assets comprise relevant knowledge, acquired skills, trainings, expertise and connections. Acquiring soft assets seems to have been part of me as I have enjoyed multiple recommendations due to my commitment. I have taken jobs that pay less compared to my educational qualifications but offer great learning platform. These most times have helped me in my subsequent job offer. Never take it for granted. You may perceive the Soft Assets as intangible, yet they are the tree that bears the Hard Assets. Would you love a high-paying job upon graduation? A Porsche? A mansion? A Rolex and a wardrobe filled with designer clothes? Good but wrong! You must, unlike many, tilt your focus away from materialism. Go for the innate things which cannot be stolen, do not expire, are priceless, unique and hence, do not need insurance.

> *Seek first the relevant knowledge and skills, and every other thing shall be added unto you.*

Hard assets are cash at hand or in the bank which you need to make a concrete decision about because money is a bad capital. Unbelievably as it might sound, the Hard Assets – luxuries and wealth would come naturally if you invest all you have in improving yourself.

Your **aspirations** and **values** are where you might like to be in the future. But the question is, what are you doing to move closer to achieving your vision? I share my experience with you when I was in high school: I always sneaked out from school, trekked a distance which lasted about 45mins to learn basic computing and engineering when my mates were attending evening classes. The passion in me for computing developed very early and I focused more on it. It no doubt affected my school grades as I finished from school with an average result, but I wasn't bothered because I was getting closer to my vision. As a college grad, you should begin to ask yourself how to build on whatever skills you have acquired but as a freshman, you should perceive school as a place where you pursue your passion and garner skills relevant to the accomplishment of your vision. The picture must not be distorted, it must be crystal clear.

> *People with vision succeed because they know where they are going.*

The **market realities** are what people will actually pay you for, what is worth the research, the energy, etc. And skills are actually paying off these days. I implore everyone to have a vision (an aim to solve a problem for society); this will help you to acquire relevant skills, stay focused, take risks (where necessary), and earn an eventual reward which translates to a meaningful life. Success in life is not entirely a matter of wealth acquisition as it is of happiness from the heart, self-satisfaction and fulfillment. Remember you are a senior to whoever does not know what you know, irrespective of their age!

These three parameters work together like the separate parts of a grid — take one out and the rest won't stand! So you see there is no point wasting your time acquiring skills that won't earn you money, is there? This I can assure you won't get you very far. I have heard many speakers talk about people following their dreams, I followed mine. However, following your dreams without being very good at it will not be too blissful after long. One sure way to upgrade your competitiveness is by upgrading your assets i.e. investing in yourself. Again I must let you know that after two years of high school, I got admission into university to study Technology (Electrical/Electronics). I spent much of the time allotted for certain general courses pursuing my passion, though I never took my tests and exams for granted. It might sound easy but it was a rigorous task which paid off with six professional certifications in IT. I offered myself through internship as a Systems Administrator/Trainer with an IT firm without salary for three years, which I perceived as a step up my career ladder though the financial gratifications were missing. I got to understand the necessity of practical experience in every profession. But I was highly compensated when leaving the firm due to my unprecedented dedication. Popular career planning advice says you should find your passion and then pursue it. But remember these philosophies have serious strengths but also huge drawbacks. They tend to presume a static world which in actual fact keeps changing.

LEARNING IN THE REAL SENSE

You need to understand that you should prioritize learning not cramming! Your soft assets should be placed on a pedestal over cash salary for the majority of your career. This principle, if followed, will enable you lead a meaningful life as well as make more money. To learn in the real sense, practice must be involved.

> *We actually learn better by doing.*

Concrete actions not plans will help you adapt to the next phase of your journey through life. Don't get me wrong, I am not saying you

...for the College Grad

shouldn't plan but take actions. Also cultivate the habit of writing down your plans and not just nursing the ideas in your head, that won't take you anywhere. I give myself a six-month target, write it down on a word pad and work hard to achieve it.

What about risks? Risk is the word many students don't want to hear. To them, risk is to incur the chance of something harmful, dangerous and detrimental. Perhaps we should remind ourselves what great risk we took coming into the world, growing up in total unconsciousness, attending elementary school across the highway, living in harsh conditions in a boarding house, going through college and eventually, earning a degree. I went through all that risk, sure what tomorrow held, and here I am better than I was. Begin to acknowledge that risk isn't really an enemy; it's a permanent part of life! In fact, one of the prerequisites of seizing breakout opportunities is by being proactively intelligent about risks.

NO RISK, NO REWARD

Where others see a red light, you'll see a green; where they see an obstacle, you see a stepping stone; where they see impossibility, you see opportunity...I tell you my friend, instead of placing faith in your ability to anticipate all that could go wrong, build up resilience to unimaginable blow up.

OUR DEFECTIVE EDUCATIONAL SYSTEM

Our educational system no doubt does not encourage creativity; it trains us to memorize facts in books written several decades ago and then regurgitate them on an exam. I was a victim of that dysfunctional system. My story is however different today because i made a choice: never to be a slave to any system. Modern professionals know that you can't acquire knowledge required to function in the modern era this way – the static way.

Knowledge required to function in the modern era is absolutely dynamic, changing every microsecond! Again, our educational system penalizes students for making mistakes. What then sets first class holders apart? Does it mean they make no mistakes? Of course they do, but **FEWER** mistakes. No one really functions in the real world until he tries, makes mistakes and tries again until eventually he clinches his goal. That was the story of Thomas Edison, the man who invented the filament bulb.

You must begin to understand there are quite a number of things school can't do for you – like coach you on how to answer interview questions or where to make the right connections. But these were the things that really worked for me and they will work for you. Some of you will literally jump at a job to clean the highway as long as the pay is good! But how relevant will that skill be in 10 years' time?

> *Yet anyone with foresight will never dismiss a job that offers tremendous learning just because the pay is low.*

...for the College Grad

Who would resist internship at an organization that offers tremendous learning and pay low? I haven't and won't! Actually, through my work time as an employee, I accepted jobs that would add value to me than pay high salary. I have no regrets though, as I have acquired all it takes to earn all I desired now. After graduation from university, I went for National Youth Service - The National Youth Service Corps (NYSC) is a one-year mandatory program undergone by graduates in Nigeria in order to learn about other cultures and contribute to community development. "Corps" members are posted to cities far from their city of origin to serve. I was posted to a school to teach Physics but I rejected the offer because I was determined to succeed in IT. I went through a difficult situation to change this offer and later found my way into NIIT (A company acclaimed to be one of the best IT Training Centres in Nigeria). The Centre Head was surprised when he saw I had a curriculum vitae which reflected my practical experience even as a youth corps. He shook hands with me and said to me: "You are welcome to NIIT". I was productive from the first day because of my previous experience in IT.

The time to set your priorities right is about NOW as you cannot afford to miss the chance to improve YOURSELF. This idea, however, does not come on a platter – may be accompanied by some discomfort, loss of a little time, social life and money and above all, some risks. But as much you're willing to take risks now to salvage the future, there are some risks you should avoid like a plague – the tarnishing of your reputation, loss of all your economic assets, or something extremely devastating.

My Now...

WHERE LEARNING ENDS

So, if no one congratulates you on the hard work you've put into your education thus far, congratulate yourself. People may tag you a boaster but you know you're not. When I talk about my grades in school, the midnight oil I burnt, the certifications I obtained and my Master's degree, do you call that a boast? I call it an encouragement to several others who are undergraduates. You are one step ahead of many but your learning has just begun. You must remind yourself constantly that graduation is not the end of learning.

> *If you compare learning to a book, your first degree is just like the preface.*

Each day presents us with an opportunity to learn more, do more and improve more on our lives. In case you do not know; the workplace is entirely different from school. The workplace is another world waiting to be explored. And in this world, every day is exam day. There, if you're not EXPANDING then you must be CONTRACTING – and that's not good for you if you ask me. If you aren't moving FORWARD you're moving BACKWARD, and that's why you must never relent in pursuing new opportunities. But most of all, view yourself as a brand. Of course there are many brands, but yours is a brand whose greatest powers lie in DIFFERENTIATION. Set yourself a-part!

Finally, "the only way to be truly satisfied is to do what you **believe** is great work. And the only way to do great work is to **love** what you do"

— *Steve Jobs.*

… for the College Grad

Part 2: Moving Forward

My Now...

Stacie J. Whitaker

Stacie J. Whitaker, Minister of the Gospel, Author, Poet, Vocalist, Inspirationalist, and Advocate for Social Equality as well as a blessed mother of three beautiful jewels; fairs as a deeply compassionate, determined and loving woman of great faith, humbly honored to serve. Currently on The Embracing Me journey, Whitaker, believes healing broken women leads to the healing and restoration of broken boys, men and eventually, families. She seeks to feed the souls of those in need of healing, restoration and inspiration through the various gifts given by God; knowing she was created to create and purposed to share each creation.

Presently attending Regent University, Whitaker seeks a Masters of Divinity and dual Masters of Art in Journalism. She holds a Bachelor degree from the University of Baltimore in Nonprofit Management. Whitaker is author of *Hell & Heaven at 8*, co-author of the *Whitaker Book of Poetry* and prior freelance writer for the Baltimore Examiners, Faith and Culture column. She is looking forward to the release of the final three books in The Embracing Me Memoir series; *16 Tears, Death at 24 und 32 The Awakening*, August 2013. Whitaker is determined to fulfill the mandate as God's chosen and elect for such a time as this, against all odds.

...for the *College Grad*

Go Swim in the Ocean: The Butterfly Syndrome
Stacie J. Whitaker-Harris

Many college students develop the "butterfly syndrome" after graduating; often feeling stuck, unready, ill-equipped, devoid of confidence and debunked by fears of failure rather than the feat of accomplishment. Go Swim in the Ocean discusses the importance of taking chances, dreaming big, pursuing goals, aiming for the moon and understanding the necessary components of riding the waves to fulfillment and success.

During the fall of 1997, a young woman with 20/20 laser sharp vision stepped onto the campus of Essex Community College with a clear concise, well thought out plan to earn a dual degree in Psychology and Foreign Language. Three years prior she attended one of Baltimore cities top high schools but took a break from school to marry and start a family. With a strict focus and deliberate moves, she determined to acquire these dual degrees with thoughts of being the first in her immediate family to matriculate from college. Her desire to raise the standard for her children, nieces, nephews, siblings and anyone in need of motivation to move beyond the brick and mortar of Baltimore's slums or to advance beyond generational poverty, kept this young woman striving towards the prize – the degree!

This bright energetic young woman began her college career hurriedly with the mindset to quickly reach the end. Each semester she carried a heavy course load which consisted of twelve to eighteen credits. Quite often, due to household and family responsibilities as well as various other commitments such as; PTA and duties from her church, she dropped classes. Continuously she overfilled her plate trying to force time to adjust to her goals causing setback after setback. For a period of time this young woman fell ill, suffered multiple losses including the death of her mother. Guidance counselors, professors, colleagues, family and friends offered the suggestion for her to postpone her education until later times but she refused. Although these life occurrences caused additional delays, she still held fast to the initial goal – completion of a college degree at all cost!

After an extended seven year attempt to acquire dual degrees, she finally settled for an Associates of Arts degree in general studies. Though not what she initially set out to accomplish, contentment filled her but satisfaction remained distant. After graduating and working full time for a financial institution for eighteen months she began reassessing her life's course. Filled with an abundance of gifts, talents and consistently acquiring new skills, this rising star set her sights on a life filled with giving, helping others improve, heal, grow, obtain education, mentorship and anything beneficial to building people mentally, socially, emotionally, economically, spiritually and financially.

...for the College Grad

Choosing music as a focal point to accomplish her purpose as well as generate an income source, she attended Morgan State University as a vocal performance major. The intent – to open a music studio and produce her own inspirational songs. After two and a half years of sharing a stage with hundreds of dynamic vocalist and musicians in Morgan States choir and performing alongside genius persons such as Bobby McFerrin another major life change forced her to drastically adjust once again. The younger of her three children grew deathly ill which caused absence from school for two semesters. This determined young motherly scholar decided to transfer to the University of Baltimore to pursue a degree in Nonprofit Management (formerly known as Community Studies and Civic Engagement). Finally, 2008 yielded a Bachelors of Arts degree from the University of Baltimore.

This spirited, woman with a passion for people has since, started her own company (having revamped even that several times), continues as social justice advocate for equality, travels the country sharing inspirational messages, teaches leadership, participates in panel discussions regarding education, homelessness, domestic violence, gang violence prevention and the preservation of family. Although starting with a mind full of **"to-do's"** and learning from various mistakes, she remained faithful, diligent, full of hope and believed that against all odds she would achieve both degrees.

Much like this young woman, many college and even high school graduates prearrange extremely methodical, stringent, well-organized and defined goals for graduation, career, marriage, business and family. Although planning for the future requires structure and diligence, too

My Now...

often rushing the process, skipping necessary steps and failed attempts toward success lead to disappointment and frustration. Yes, the young woman spoken of is ME. As the first person in my immediate family to graduate with a college degree while remaining driven on the educational path to become **DOCTOR** Stacie J. Whitaker-Harris, I offer this advice:

1) Set goals!
2) Make plans
3) Be open to advice
4) Know when to ask for assistance (AND DO IT)
5) Be committed to excellence but remain flexible
6) Capitalize on resources at your institution, on the web, in your community, from your place of employment (this may require research on your part – do the work!)
7) Seek mentorship for personal and professional development
8) DO NOT Rush – take your time and do things right the first time
9) Know your limitations so that you do not become overwhelmed
10) Most importantly, DO NOT QUIT!

Maximize the college experience. Rise to the top of the mountain! Conquer! Accomplish! Strive! However, enjoying every moment, every opportunity and exposure to new experiences – absorb the wisdom of those who have traveled the same road prior to your arrival. Take chances.

...for the College Grad

Soar, for I am the Eagle

As I sit peering through the rectangular shaped window, I see the purity of life; I feel the crispness in the air. Watching the hills of thick white smoky clouds paint the ocean blue sky invigorates and motivates me. As I sit listening to the roar of the engine, I hear the earth speaking loudly carrying frustrations away with every thrust of its voice. I hear the Angels singing praises and calm is upon my being. I am soaring in places I only dreamed of and I am as free as the birds, yet with invisible wings I still fly high. High above each think soft bundle of cotton and the eagles are no match for the distance I've flown. The air is no match for my deliberate push against it as each wind only assists in my elevation. I am not stagnant in the air flying aimlessly but I soar purposefully toward my destination.

And yes, as I climb higher into the air the suns warmth at times seek to obliterate my journey, for it beats hard against my invisible wings and it dries up the wind leaving only steam. The sun is my guiding light yet it to seeks to take me off course. But again, the sun is no match for the fire that burns within. I soak up its warmth and increase in strength with a passionate intensity. I intend to stay in the air not by chance but by choice. I meet each cloud with a hello and quickly say goodbye as I rise above it. I look the eagle in its eyes and glean from it the inspiration to go higher. I howl too with the wind and sound my own alarms letting the Angels know I am aware of their presence. And no matter what, I forge full speed ahead towards the sun at first afraid of disintegrating but then realizing I gain strength from the sun as it sets the tone for my path.

My Now...

I increase in every way clearing a path for those behind me. As I rise they rise too. As I conquer, they too conquer. As I shine my rays give light to their paths and I am reminded, someone, those invisible wings are those who came before me. Those winds that blow strong are also the arms of the Angels guiding me and pushing me to stay the course. Those clouds were protection, blocking my vision from seeing those things that could harm. Those loud sounds were not distractions but they represent two parts; **One** – The warrior Angels on the other side of the clouds fighting on my behalf and at the same time screaming to say, "Keep going. You're almost there". **Two** – The sound of victory for those who traveled this same road and now sit in the distance applauding my ascension into great places. My reward is beautiful. There in places I ONLY DREAMED of lies the heart of my existence. This existence is the ability to live freely in the face of every adverse effect of things that I ONLY THOUGHT were there to keep me from reaching my destination but instead they guided my flight, helping me to soar high above the clouds – going a distance unknown to the common one.

...for the *College Grad*

My Now...

Sharon A. Myers

Sharon A. Myers is the Founder and Executive Director of Moovin4ward Presentations, a youth empowerment company that facilitates leadership and success workshops for high school and college students around the country. She is the co-developer of the student program, **Journey to Success: Personal Success Strategic Plan (PSSP) Program**, which is based on the book *Mapping Your Journey to Success: Six Steps for Personal Planning.*

Sharon is the author of *Slumber Party, Critical Competence,* and *90 Tips for the First 90 Days.* She is also a contributing author in *My Vision, My Plan, My Now* and *My Now for the Entrepreneur.*

sharon@moovin4ward.com
www.Moovin4ward.com
www.Journey2Success.com
Tweet @moovin4ward

...for the *College Grad*

Keep On Rolling!

Sharon A. Myers

When my oldest daughter was a toddler, she skipped the crawling stage. Not metaphorically, but literally. No matter how many times I propped her up on her hands and knees to show her how, she would fall to her belly, choose her destination, and ROLL towards it.

As the months passed, she got faster at it... traveling faster than any crawling baby around. So fast, in fact, that she'd sometimes roll off course and hit an obstacle that she wasn't aiming for—the fireplace, ottoman, or wall. At those times, she would simply stop rolling, raise her head to see where she was, reposition her body, and then KEEP ON ROLLING!

That was 18 years ago. I'm actually just now seeing the life lessons in her actions. As you commence into your life with college behind you, I'd like to encourage you to **Keep On Rolling.**

Consider doing the following:
- Skin a Cat
- Reposition
- Slow Your Roll
- Get Propped Up
- Keep Moving
- Stay Motivated

My Now...

Skin a Cat

The old saying goes, "there's more than one way to skin a cat." Now, I've never skinned a cat to know this to be true; but I get the point. Basically, there's more than one way to do things. The beaten path isn't always the only way to reach your destination. It might be easier, but what fun is that? How much more exciting must it be to roll rather than merely crawl? Everyone does that!

In life, sometimes you'll find that you learn and experience more when you are determined to create your <u>own</u> way of doing things. Don't just follow the crowd. And by all means, don't let anyone tell you that there is **<u>only</u>** one way to do something; especially if you have a vision of a way to do it differently. Go ahead and skin a cat; give it a try.

At the same time, expect that there will always be people in your life that will tell you that you're "doing it all wrong." If it comes from people you trust, by all means take the easier and proven path. But don't be afraid to skin that cat. After all, you're a college graduate, so it's okay to take an "educated guess." Keep on rolling!

Reposition

Occasionally, you may swerve off course and hit an untended bump in your path. It happens to the best of us. And for the greatest of us, it happens often. You may be well on your way to your destination, when... BAM! You hit an obstacle. What happens next is what defines who you are.

Option number one would be to give up. Go back to where you started and stay put. Do absolutely nothing else. Or, you may go for option number two—my toddler's choice: check where you are and assess the damage. Figure out how to get to where you intended to go from where you are. Reposition and continue on your journey. Remember, you survived college. Regardless of what you told your friends and family, I'm more than certain that you banged a few obstacles while you were there. Keep on rolling!

Slow Your Roll

For some, rushing to reach a destination is the primary reason for hitting so many obstacles. Slow down! Don't be in such a hurry to get there. It's amazing how many people believe that as soon as they graduate from college, they will immediately land their dream job, meet and marry their dream mate, purchase their dream home, and have their American dream life... all by the age of 25. Really?

Not everyone will tell you this (or maybe you've heard it a million times and didn't listen), but time is on your side. If you live life as a race, you aren't living... you're racing! Watching my daughter roll around the floor was hilarious, especially when she was in a hurry. It always seemed to take twice as long to get where she wanted to go. Why? Because she would carelessly get more unintended bumps and bangs. When this happened, she would get frustrated and lose focus of where she was trying to go.

So, take your time, slow your roll, stay on task, stay focused, and reach your destination without excessive bruises. You'll get there. Keep on rolling!

Get Propped Up

My daughter is now a freshman in college. Her toddler rolling phase continued through her teen years. Well, not literally, but metaphorically. Throughout the years, I continued to try to "prop her up" and get her to go the way I thought was best. But she consistently skinned the cat her way... until recently. She has finally learned that sometimes it's okay to ask for and/or accept help.

When you graduate from college, you may feel like you are now "all knowing," but you aren't. The sooner you learn that, the better off you'll be. I can almost guarantee that there are people around you that are willing, ready, and able to prop you up to get you started in the right direction.

However, be careful of *only* wanting to be propped up before making a move. This can be bad because without a few bruises of your own, you don't build up your personal library of learned lessons. These lessons, or bruises, will help you to make your own decisions in your future. Then keep on rolling!

Keep Moving

Understand that you didn't make it this far in your life by standing still. Maybe you started out with one destination in mind, and thanks to unforeseen circumstances, you ended up some place else entirely. Or just maybe, you are *exactly* where you wanted to be. Good for you. The point is that you didn't remain at a standstill—you were moving. I will assume that where you stand right now is not where you started. You were motivated to move forward. And it's even better when you are self-motivated.

To be self-motivated means to be able to get things done without being directed by others. Basically, you have to be your own cheerleader. Some people can cheer themselves on with ease. I've spent many of times in the mirror giving myself a pep talk when I needed it. But I recognize that not everyone has that capability. You need to identify what will give you the extra boost of motivation that you need to finish strong. Researchers have identified several internal and external motivators that give us the desire to move forward.

Internally motivated people are driven by how they _feel_ about their own actions. These may include:

- *Achievement*: the desire to work for the challenge
- *Competence*: the desire to master a job or do your best
- *Belief*: the desire to uphold personal values

Externally motivated people are driven by what they _receive_ for their actions, such as money or recognition. These may include:

- *Power*: the desire to seek control or drive others
- *Affiliation*: the desire to be with other people while achieving goals
- *Position*: the desire to "move up the ladder"
- *Hero*: the desire to be like someone you admire or shine in their eyes

Once you've identified what motivates you, use it to your advantage. Keep on rolling.

Stay Motivated

Finding what motivates you is one thing, staying motivated is something totally different. It is often a struggle because our drive is constantly attacked by negative thoughts or anxiety about the future. Most normal people will lose motivation at some point in life; it's all part of growth. Here are a few tips to help you stay motivated:

Dismiss fear.

Often fear can cripple your energy and stop you from feeling motivated. When this happens, remind yourself that fear is just an ungrounded feeling. Then dismiss it. You will feel more motivated once you've moved beyond your fear.

Hurdle challenges.

Often when we face challenges we feel defeated and want to give in. If you remind yourself at these times that every meaningful success involves many challenges, then you will suddenly see that your current challenge is in fact a sign of progress. It's all in how you look at it.

Commit to completion.

Often times I have so many goals that I want to achieve that I lose the motivation to achieve any of them. Make a commitment to complete what you start without overwhelming yourself with too much at once.

Chance it.

A loss of motivation can come when we feel paralyzed in having to do something outside of our comfort zone. When you chance it, you are daring yourself to do something out of the box that you aren't certain of. When you succeed on a chance, you will kick your motivation into overdrive!

Finally

You've achieved a great accomplishment. You've graduated from college. Many have tried and failed to get to this point. As the old saying goes, "if it were easy, everyone would be doing it." Well everyone is not doing it. But you skinned a cat and made it happen.

But as many of the other authors in this book have mentioned, you are really just getting started.

My Now...

Set your mind on your next accomplishment, then drop to your belly and roll towards it. You may hit a bump or two, or even three, along the way; but stay motivated. At every bump, raise your head to see where you are; reposition your body towards your destination, then Keep on Rolling.

...for the College Grad

My Now...

Mark W. Wiggins

Mark "The Speaker Man" Wiggins, an International speaker, trainer, author and entrepreneur is the CEO of Xtreme Effort Speaking. He has held leadership and management positions within several national retail companies, such as Foot Locker, Eddie Bauer, and Levi Strauss & Co. He has trained corporate, community, and association leaders in the Washington, DC area on the topics of customers, leadership and human performance.

He is the author of *Permission to Succeed: the Only Person Who Needs to Give it is You*; *MTXE the Formula for Success*; and more. He is also one of the featured authors of the book, *My Vision, My Plan, My NOW!*

Get my information right now! Text the word "Speakerman" to 90210.

Email: Mark@markthespeakerman.com

...for the College Grad

Moving Without the Ball

Mark Wiggins

There is a concept in basketball called "moving without the ball."

It refers to what you do when the spotlight is *not* on you, or when you don't have the ball in your possession. Think about it, there is only one ball, and 4 other players on offensive who don't have it in their hands. Even if they get it they only keep it for so long. There is the shot clock, 5 seconds rule, and the 3 seconds in the paint rule. So, while one person has the ball, the other 4 are doing their part to get open, or get in a better position to score. So over the course of a 40 minute game, you could conceivably only have the ball in your hands a total of 5-6 minutes a game. What will you do the other 35 minutes? Move without the ball of course and play defense. Therefore, learning how to move without the ball is a very important skill. Since getting open and moving without the ball is a skill, it can be learned.

Most times during the game, when you are on offense, you are working to get open for an opportunity to score or make a play. Moving to the ball requires a lot more work than it does to actually have the ball.

Think about it... you run around, cut, work to get open and when you get the ball, the focus is now on you.

My Now...

What will you do?

You can become a triple threat; you can pass the ball, drive to the net or shoot from where you are. In either case, a decision will have to be made, and hopefully you have prepared for this moment. Your moment may be brief, but you have to make something happen. If you have worked hard on your skills and done the prep work and practice, you should be fine with what you do next. As a matter of fact, it should almost be a reaction, not a thought.

Let me put this in musical terms, Louis Armstrong was asked how he could play his trumpet with such ease and grace. He replied "I practice; practice and practice, and then I just blow." His point is that he has worked so hard at developing his skills that when it is his time to play, he can just perform and not think about it.

Reggie Miller was one of the NBA's greatest at moving without the ball. He would run around for what seemed like minutes to get open (but in actually it was only seconds) and then he would take a shot. His defenders would often give up because they were not ready for the physical and mental punishment they would take trying to guard him. So essentially, when he got the ball, opponents were tired out and Miller's next move would be met with little resistance.

Now, let me make this relevant to the College Grad. Moving without the ball simply means *doing what you need to when the spotlight is **not** on you and working hard until you find the opportunity to put yourself in position to win.*

In other words you need to learn how to NETWORK.

Let's talk about that...*dictionary.com* defines Networking as:

a supportive system of sharing information and services among individuals and groups having a common interest.

Most people think that networking is about the "hook-up", like knowing the cafeteria workers so they give you an extra scoop of mashes potatoes for free. While that type of "hook-up" has its purpose, it will not necessarily get you the job or internship you need to reach your goals. Networking is a little more sophisticated and if done correctly, you can find yourself with opportunities to walk through open doors that you did not know existed.

Networking is not what someone can do for you; it is about what YOU CAN DO FOR SOMEONE ELSE. How can you increase your value to someone and have him or her want to keep you around or to be a resource for them?

In sales, the easiest lead is a referral. A referral does not guarantee that you will get the business, but it does increase the likelihood that you will get the opportunity to present yourself and earn the business. So, just being out of college you need to think like a sales professional, and the product for sale is YOU. Here are my starting line-up of 5 of things you need to know to maximize your networking, and to "sell yourself" more effectively:

My Now...

1. **Join professional organizations related to your industry**, and join social organizations for the causes you support. This is a very good way to meet people that speak your language and will be more likely to support you or mentor you as you learn your way around your industry. People get to learn about others in a familiar environment, and since you have some of the same interests, it makes starting conversations easier and less stressful. Have a growth mindset when you join, not a fixed mindset. A growth mindset is open to learning and will to do what it takes to gain knowledge and can take coaching well. The fixed mindset is basically thinks it "knows it all" and is less likely to make a strong positive impact on others.

2. **Take a leadership role in your organizations.** Don't just join and pay dues and go to meetings. Look for ways to get involved and to show off your skill set and abilities. You never know who is watching and more importantly who they know. Remember networking is about what you can do for others. If someone sees something in your leadership style, or your work habits, they could pick up the phone and open doors for you. Think about that, you are just doing what you do best, and someone takes an interest in you and makes a connection. It's almost like you are auditioning for a role (but you don't know which one) so you just perform at your best to be prepared for anything...maybe even the leading role! You are not asking for a handout, you want to earn that referral or connection, and the best way still to do that is by HARD WORK.

3. **Learn about your work environment**, before you make moves. Coaches love new talent; however, the team is slow to accept the newcomer. This is a very important point for you to remember as you transition into your new career. You may come in and actually be managing people that have:

    A. Had a job there for years or,

B. Be much older than you.

They do not take kindly to change. They may not question your ability, but they will question your motives. Look at it from their point of view, you're young, hungry, and trying to make an impression. Yes, you are the new talent and the Mangers / coaches may love you, but the team/co-workers, are slow to accept you.

Make sure you learn the lay of the land. That's not to say you don't do your job, but understand they may actually know more than you. Engage them and learn what they do best and be willing to show them that you are there to help not only the company succeed, but also help your team succeed as well. It's hard to go into battle and not know the capabilities of your enemy. You must study them, learn what makes them tick, and understand where there maybe differences…then learn to ease those fears. Who knows? You just might learn a thing or two about your new job, from someone that used to be in your shoes.

4. **Reposition yourself.** It's all about finding new opportunities and looking for openings that allow you to contribute to your team, learn new skills, and broaden your network. Some people get in a job and just do that job. One of my favorite movies is "Coming to America" with Eddie Murphy, where he was working at this burger place, mopping the floor but did not like it. An employee told him there was hope, because he was mopping the floor once and now he was very happy to be working the fries, and was going to move up to a new position. Sounds funny, but the concept is the same. Learn what you can, be willing to move to new opportunities and open some new doors for yourself. The people you may be managing or working with could be older than you or on the job longer, but you will have to earn their respect by being willing to work.

This brings me to my last point in moving without the ball:

5. **Work Smart & Hard**

   As glamorous and effortless as it seemed to watch Reggie Miller move without the ball to get open, one could easily overlook the work he put in to make it look that easy. Often people overlook or fail to take seriously the work that it takes to be good. There is no replacing hard work. There are no short cuts and there is no quick way to improve your skill set other than by hard work. This will include trainings, briefings, travel, and extra assignments. All of these things have to take place in order for you to look effortless when you do what you do best.

My old college coach said, "Always work to improve, never work to maintain."

What he means is, is if you are going to work at something, why not get better?

Why not read books, go to trainings and seminars, get coaching, get a mentor, or do whatever it takes to get what you want? People say you should work smart not hard. I used to buy into that, but I never really understood, why I would not also need to work hard. The actual application should be...work smart in what you are doing and when you figure it out, work hard to be more productive. That's like lifting weights... you can get a good work out in the gym and sling a bunch of weight or do a bunch of cardio, but if you don't have a plan for what you want to improve upon, you won't see the results you want. However, if you plan and focus on an area, say your abs, and you go to the gym and focus and work hard on your abs; you will get the results you desire. Therefore, you need to work smart **AND** hard to get the result you want.

I told of group of college bound athletes once, "I wish someone had told me that what I did as an athlete to get into college was not good enough to keep me there."

So I am telling you the MY NOW College Graduate...

What you did after college to get your first job will not be enough to keep you employed there.

You will have to WORK HARD to stay there.

Let's review my starting 5 points to moving without the ball:

1) Join professional Organizations
2) Take leadership roles in those organizations
3) Learn about your work environment
4) Reposition yourself
5) Work Smart AND Hard

When the buzzer Sounds

NBA playoffs 2013, Game 6, Heat Vs. Spurs in Miami. It's the fourth quarter and the Heat are down...if they lose this game, they lose the series because the Spurs were up 3 games to 2.

The start of the 4th quarter the Heat seemed unable to mount any type of a comeback. The game had gotten so desperate, that the Heat

My Now...

fans started leaving the game. Time was winding down but the Heat kept fighting, Lebron was performing like the MVP, again.

With minutes left, the Heat seemed to be on a roll, the Spurs were reeling and rocking, but holding on, they needed just a few more seconds and it would have been their 5th title...adding them to the ranks of the Lakers, Celtics and Bulls with 5 or more titles. Down 3 with seconds left, the Heat miss a shot, the ball is bouncing around, Chris Bosh, grabs the loose ball, Ray Allen, sprints to the corner, Chris passes the ball to the deadliest three-point shooter in the game, open in the corner, just as the clock clicks zeros, Allen is able to launch a scud missile with laser locked guidance, nothing but net, the buzzer sounds and the game is tied, NOW what?

OVERTIME!

I will not bore you with what happened in overtime but the bottom line the Heat win game six and seven and bring home back-to-back NBA World championships.

Most of my writings include some sports reference. I have played or coached basketball for most of my life. I was fortunate to have played in college. People say that your career is over before you know it, and you then are relegated to playing in work leagues, city leagues, or just giving up the sport all together. When I started playing, the end seemed so far away. I was able to jump high, run fast, run all day.

NOW?

...for the *College Grad*

I am lucky to run at all, hit a few shots, and I play in the old man league where layups are frowned upon and the long range jumper is praised.

So what about this buzzer thing? The buzzer is a signal to everyone that something about to change. It is either the ending or the beginning of something. It could be practice or the game, it does not matter. When that familiar sound comes everyone knows that there is a change in what needs to happen next. The question is...are you prepared for what comes next?

Let's bring this back to you, the College Graduate. You started college with the bright eyes and uncertainty, you knew that this process would be a grind; you would have to work hard, or even work two jobs to make this thing happen. You knew that the experience you received would help you in your next steps in life. These last years, where the slowest fastest years of your life. All of a sudden, or it seemed like that, you looked up and the buzzer was sounding, for you that buzz was graduation. The signification of the end of something, your college career, and the beginning of something else, the rest of your lives as college graduates...what NOW?

Reggie Miller, Lebron James and Ray Allen, spent countless hours sharping their skills, grinding, waiting for that moment when the buzzer sounds to either start the game or end the game. Either way, they have prepared. So, your Buzzer has sounded, pomp and circumstance has played and you have tossed your hat into the air. NOW, as you await the next buzzer to sound and you start your next phase in life, take time to

My Now...

work on your skills, take every advantage you can get to prepare you for that moment when you get off the bench and get your chance to shine. Learn how to position yourself for success, and above all, commit to working hard and you will be able to achieve the success you desired and dreamed about when you stared college, wait….. What's that I hear? It's a buzzer... GAME TIME!

NOW get off the bench and get in the starting line-up of life!

...for the College Grad

My Now...

Lesa Day

Lesa Day is an internationally known speaker, author, and parenting family coach, who is sought out by parents, education and childcare organizations worldwide. With her top selling book in hand, "How to Get Your Child to Say Yes! I can! and I will!", this Atlanta based speaker transforms the hearts and minds of our youth and empowers them to reach their greatest potential. Lesa Day has appeared on radio and television broadcasts nationwide and is the founder and CEO of We Win Life Coaching, an empowerment and coaching firm dedicated to bring the best out of individuals, companies and organizations. You can connect with her online at the following links:

Facebook: Parenting Family Coach
Twitter: ParentsNFamily
LinkedIn: Lesa Day
Website: www.yesIcanandIwill.com

...for the College Grad

Success! How Bad Do You Want It?

Lesa Day

I have a t-shirt that says in bold letters on the front, "Sometimes it's not how good you are, but how bad you want it." As a college graduate you are about to start a new chapter in your life. Helen Keller said "Life is a daring, bold adventure or nothing at all" and I've lived my life as an adventure. Whether I'm sky diving at 15,000 feet, swimming with dolphins in Australia, coaching people in China, or empowering a child to put his best effort in whatever he chooses to do, I've determined to live life to its fullest. Your success is determined by the choices you make on a daily basis. It's about the collective decisions you make throughout your life. It's a journey! You need to think of living life as running a marathon vs. the 100 meter sprint.

Now is the time for you to create your bucket list. Don't wait, do it now! Even if you don't take any immediate action steps to accomplish anything on your list take out a piece of paper and create your bucket list now. Studies have shown over and over again that people who write down their dreams and goals are more likely to realize them. When I wrote my dream list in my early 20's I was amazed after years had gone by how many of the things on it I had already accomplished.

My Now...

Growing up in a small town with a graduating class of 123 students I had dreams to travel the world. I thought there was so much to learn from other cultures. I believed that life was an adventure to experience. I considered the world my classroom. What was once a dream became a reality. I have been blessed to travel all over the globe from South America, Greece, Turkey, Australia, the Caribbean Islands, and all over the U.S. and eastern Canada.

But let me share something I believe is even more significant. The people who I have met along the way have given me insurmountable insight into success and have shown me what it means to be truly happy in life. Whether I'm working with upper management employees from Beijing; coaching individuals on leadership and team building in the technology industry in Cheng Du and Singapore; or interviewing high school athletes with character traits worth duplicating, I have as much to learn from them as they do from me.

When you seek to grow and improve people will come into your life to help you. Purposely make yourself aware of those people and seek them out to spend as much time with them as you can. I'll never forget when I met Charlie "Tremendous" Jones, the author of "Life is Tremendous" in my early twenties. He told me, "The two things that will determine where you will be five years from now are the people you meet and the books that you read."

Since that time I have become an avid reader and I'm choosey about the books I read. I want to read books that inspire me, teach me, and challenge me to be a better person. I also make a point to seek people whom I respect to mentor me. As I grew in my career I developed new programs, built teams, and received awards. But here is what I realized early in my career, there's great power in building your team. You were not meant to do this alone. The people on your team vary depending on what you're trying to accomplish. They are people who can mentor you in areas you wish to grow in or can be people who have talents you need to accomplish a particular goal.

When I wrote my first book I built a team of men and women who had various strengths to evaluate my work. I wanted a diverse group of people with a diverse range of skills who would give me gut level, honest feedback on the content in my book. After years of building strong connections I had a dedicated team of people, including skilled editors and skilled marketers, working on my book with me. The book turned out to be an award winning parenting book the following year.

As you grow in your career there will be great leaders to help you along the way. Latch onto them. Gain as much wisdom from them as you can. Don't look at others as competitors but instead view them as valuable contributors in your journey to becoming the best you can be. When you give your best and continue to grow to become the person you're called to be you will rise to success. Ask yourself, why are you doing it? What is driving you to pursue the particular career you've chosen? If you were a multi-millionaire would you still be working in the profession you've chosen to pursue? If not, what would you be doing?

You have passion inside of you for something. What is it? There's a reason it's there and you've been given talents to pursue it. I have a

My Now...

passion to teach and equip others to go after their dreams. I desire to help individuals develop solid leadership skills, and to empower them to use their talents to make a difference in the world around them. I have a passion for leadership that requires great character and personal ethics. As I became aware of this it gave me direction on my career as a personal coach. There are many different types of life coaches out there, but I was able to hone in on areas of leadership and character development that make my offerings unique and applicable across generations. I'm either equipping children for adulthood by coaching them in life skills that teach good habits and character or coaching business owners in leadership to build a better company.

I recall recently talking with a senior who had played varsity baseball the last 3 years of school and his position had always been third base. This year he ended up playing first. I asked him why? He explained to me that as much as he preferred playing third base that he was the only one on the team with the ability to play first base and the needs of the team came first. In his early years he had some exceptional coaches who lead their team to championship seasons. They always reinforced the importance of the team over the individual. During those beginning years of sports phenomenal character was being built that will take that young man far in his adulthood as he pursues his dreams and goals. He's always had a heart for the team and this has made him a great leader.

I saw a highly competitive freshman wrestler who had been a New England champion since he was 5 years old start his high school season in a weight class at 138 lbs. - which is 15 lbs. less than his normal weight. This young man was slim, very muscular, and had very little body fat. He could have easily wrestled at 152 lbs. weight class. I interviewed him and asked him why he chose to wrestle in the lower weight class? He shared with me he did it for two reasons. First, the young man who wanted to wrestle at 152 lbs. was a friend and he didn't want to ruin the friendship knowing he would beat him if they had to competitively wrestle in that weight class. The other reason was there was no one else on the team who had the discipline to lose the weight to make the 138 lbs. weight bracket so he sacrificed whatever was necessary to fill that need. When I found out what that entailed I was in awe. Here was a 14 year old boy determined to make weight each week, putting friendship and the team before his wants and needs. As I pondered that I thought to myself, if this young man has this kind of personal discipline and dedication to a team he's headed for success in whatever he chooses to pursue in life. He inspires me!

One of my favorite books written on success in business is "Good to Great" by Jim Collins. I highly recommend it as a must read! He teaches at Harvard and did six years of research on the top successful companies in the U.S. In the book he explains what made each company go from good to great. In order for a company to be considered "great" Jim Collins had tough criteria for them to meet, "A company had to generate cumulative stock returns that exceeded the general stock market by at least three times over 15 years—and it had to be a leap independent of its industry." Out of all the companies in the U.S. there were only 11 companies he could find to meet this criteria - and the names would surprise you. Walgreens, Kroger, and Kimberly Clark were on the list. As he dug deeper into each of those companies he saw some significant similarities that caused them to have long term success. One of the characteristics that shined so brightly was their understanding of leadership. You can be the smartest person around, create things that could bring you millions of dollars, but if you can't effectively work with people you or your company won't reach its full potential.

You could be a natural visionary but you need people on your team who can see your vision and then plan the necessary steps to bring it to fruition. To do this you must have the people skills and leadership skills to build a good team. Being able to connect with people and understand the power of great, authentic leadership will allow you to succeed in whatever you choose to pursue in life.

So as you go after your dreams and work at attaining your goals consider the passion inside of you and why you're doing it. Then create good habits by doing the following:

- Write your bucket list now, keep it close by and continue add to it!
- Decide to become an avid reader to grow professionally and personally.
- Create a circle of mentors in your life who will push you to reach the next level and keep you accountable.
- Use your gifts and talents to make the world better. As much as you have individual dreams you would like to accomplish remember it's not all about you. You are making an impact in the world based on the talents you've been given. It's your choice as to whether it's positive or negative.

My top reading recommendations:
1. The 7 Habits of Highly Effective People by Stephen Covey
2. Good to Great by Jim Collins
3. The Greatest Miracle in the World by Og Mandino
4. Why Aren't You More Like Me by Everett T. Robinson
5. Skill with People by Les Giblin
6. The E-Myth by Michael Gerber

Bibliography: http://www.jimcollins.com/article_topics/articles/good-to-great.html

My Now...

B. Nate Smith

Nate is a graduate of Norfolk State University, Norfolk, Virginia where he pursued his B.A. in Political Science/Pre-Law and his M.A. in Secondary Education-History. Nate received his second M.A. degree in Administration and Supervision from the University of Phoenix and is in his final year as a doctoral student with Nova Southeastern University, Orlando, Florida, pursuing his Ed.D. in Higher Education Leadership.

Denoting the need to speak to the positive aspects of men, Nate authored a profound book entitled, *"5 Ways to Affirm a Man: Character, Communication, Care, Commitment, and Consistency"*. It is a refreshing and skillfully written guide on understanding, learning, valuing, appreciating and affirming men and improving their behavioral tendencies and social responses. The following books will be published by Nate as of fall 2013.

1. Nate-Isms!
2. Nate's Notions: You Matter
3. Men, Beware of a Woman If...

Mr. Smith can be reached at: b.nathanielsmith@yahoo.com

Preparation for Excellence: A 5 Step Process

B. Nate Smith

As a person, you cannot allow others to set the limits of your success. You must be fearless, aggressive, and active in managing, molding, and modifying the change that you desire. To that cause, this section is designed for those individuals who aspire towards excellence. You abhor average, you detest mediocrity and you absolutely ignore the status quo. You are an adventurer, seek opportunities for advancement, and are not afraid to approach new challenges with an inquisitive cognition! Have you closed the book yet? No? Great! Then let's get you calibrated for excellence.

Preparation for Excellence consists of five components that will position you to possess the best that your skills, experience, and talent can afford you. The five components are *Preparation, Planning, Sacrifice, Strategy (Goals),* and *Fulfillment*. Each component will be examined, explained and expressed in such a way that you will be able to employ the tenets to your advantage. The first component is preparation.

My Now...

PREPARATION

Before reading further, please answer the following question: What does the term 'preparation' mean to you?

_____

_____

Now that you have had time to provide your own personal reflection, get up from your current reclined position, walk over to a mirror and look directly into it and say the following words: *'AS I THINK, SO I AM! AS I THINK, SO I AM! AS I THINK, SO I AM!'*

Preparation requires you to realize that a paradigm must occur. Think about it! You are a college graduate who is positioning himself/herself for the competitive advantage in corporate society where change is inevitable. What makes you more valuable, visible and visceral than the next person? Your preparation!

Preparation requires you to:

- Acknowledge your limitations but do not submit to them. Oftentimes, individuals fail to take a personal inventory of who they are. Failing to do so may provide you with an unrealistic reality of who you are.
- Assess all of your opportunities and determine which are the most feasible and accessible based upon your current talent, skill, and influence.

- Analyze your competition. By studying them, you also learn valuable things about yourself.
- Ascribe to the mental work that is required which differentiates you from all others. Compose a list of your strengths, weaknesses, opportunities for growth, and the threats that may be associated with your success (SWOT Analysis).
- Accept the fact that there will be pros and cons that you will wrestle with during your preparation phase.
- Accelerate at your own pace. Do not allow the preparation phase to exhaust you to the point of giving up. Be mindful, YOU are not average!
- Ask yourself the following questions: *Who will I need to assist me? Who will my decisions affect? What is it that I want to accomplish? When will I meet my goal? What time frame is necessary? Why am I doing this?*

At this point, I would encourage to you to stop reading this chapter, put this book down, get up and get you something to drink and grab a snack...that comment is only for those who are not ready for a deeper depth in the dimensions of learning how to establish your destiny! For all others, dismiss those hunger pains and read on!!! The second component is *planning*.

PLANNING

Before reading further, please answer the following question: What does the term 'planning' mean to you?

My Now...

_____

_____

I am not sure what you wrote down but if it did not incorporate the use of your hands...then your response is completely WRONG! Planning is the phase in which you must **get your hands dirty.** So shake off any inhibitions, identify your goals and conduct an inventory of your resources.

Planning requires you to:

- Realize that you have to do some physical work. In other words, you must conduct research, establish the proper rapport, be able to relate to others, and be willing to revise your efforts to meet the expectations of your overall goals.
- Realize that you must accept all of the responsibility that comes along with your *Preparation for Excellence.*
- Revise your problem solving techniques based upon your prior and current experiences. Consider the following:
    - state your current situation as a problem
    - secure information from credible sources that will change your current situation
    - solutions, solutions, solutions...brainstorm for the best solution
    - select the best solution and apply it and then examine the outcome(s)

- o strategize...if the outcomes from the solution chosen are not applicable and does not yield you the best results, scrap it and start over
- Research your geographical, economical, philosophical, spiritual, and familial ideologies as they will be relevant to your next component which is *sacrifice*
- Rank the internal and external distractions. At all cost, avoid negative people and negative situations. They are a weight that invariably will hold you back from your goals
- Rate your resources and review your options again! Use your resources wisely and often

It is now assessment time. You have made it through the *preparation* phase and you have just completed the *planning* phase. The next component is that of *sacrifice*. It is the shortest and simplest component that is required in your *Preparation For Excellence*. If you are unwilling to sacrifice your time, your talent, and remain tenacious, you can put this book down and take a nap and sleep your life away. Yet, if you are ready for the next step, then keep all arms and legs inside this moving vehicle at all times. The next component will be a bumpy ride!

SACRIFICE

Before reading further, please answer the following question: What does the term 'sacrifice' mean to you?

_____

My Now...

It is my hope that you were honest with your reply to the question above as sacrifice is all those things that we as humans despise doing. Due to our innate, narcissistic nature, we have the propensity to want, want, want and have our needs met as opposed to having to give, give, give, to meet the needs of others.

That is what sacrifice is all about ladies and gentlemen...relinquishing your needs and desires now to ascertain a greater value at a later date. Let's explore the concept of sacrifice a little further.

Sacrifice requires you to:

Count the cost. If you can identify the areas that you are willing to sacrifice now, for your future benefit, then you are willing to count the cost. Not everyone will immediately support, sponsor, or even subscribe to your action plan yet you have to know who you are and be secure in the decisions that you are making.

- Calculate the risk factor(s). You have to realize that you are making yourself vulnerable to the possibility of living your life to your fullest potential. In addition, you must realize that you will be in a position to learn new things, be exposed to a diversity of cultures, and must be willing to adapt in various atmospheres. You will be vulnerable but do not mistake that for being venerable!

- Consider the adjustments that you will be making now and in the future. In biology you learned that you have five senses, touch, sight, taste, smell, and hearing. All of these will be impacted as you sacrifice for your future.
- Confront your fears. Do not fear, fear. You cannot fail at this because you have never done it this way before so in essence, stop contemplating what if's in a negative way and just go for yours!

In the beginning of this chapter I informed you that there were five components in your *Preparation For Excellence*. We have discussed *preparation, planning, and sacrifice*. You have endured through the most difficult phases and you only have two more to read through. Let's keep moving as I can tell that your momentum has intensified and your inquisitiveness is heightened. The fourth phase is *strategy*.

STRATEGY (GOALS)

Before reading further, please answer the following question: What does the term 'strategy' mean to you?

_____

_____

This is the phase in which you get to bring in all of your philosophical and intellectual connotations and ideologies. You get to use everything from your prior knowledge and experiences from that of your collaborative research experiences to the examples of success and failures from your own family dynamics. This is the phase in which your cognition is fully engaged.

Strategy requires you to:

- Devise your strategy plan in such a way that you map out specific assessment points and you incorporate a timeline. Goals must be detailed, specific, and measurable. If you have ever utilized a project management action plan document, you know exactly what I mean. If you have never utilized one in the past, you need to Google a sample project management outline or timeline. It will definitely be advantageous for you at this phase.
- Describe each strategy, step-by-step. This is not an over-night process but if you lay out your strategy in detail, it can make for a less stressful night.
- Diagram what each step will look like, in your perspective. If your first step incorporates looking for employment in an urban area with metro access, then your diagram should incorporate all of your chosen urban areas, the distance to the nearest metro, the surrounding shops, markets, and eateries, and the local businesses and establishments that appeal to you. Make modifications where necessary.
- Devote the time needed to this phase because as you plan for your future, you are living in your now. Remember, during this phase change and transition is continuous. Hone your time management skills.
- Deadlines must be set. You will need to schedule phone conferences, in-person meetings, and conduct reconnaissance

of what your future will entail. Be flexible, be frugal, but be focused. Network like crazy!
- Differentiate between ambiguity and ambition. The two can be one in the same.

I can assure you that one of two key feelings are permeating your being at this present time. The first is that of pure excitement in knowing that these steps are applicable in helping you to ascertain your future goals. The other potential feeling could be despair as you realize you are nowhere near where you should be in reaching your goals. Not to fear...be it excitement or despair, you are at the final phase which is *fulfillment*. This is the celebration stage so I need you to not only hang in there but to realize that this is the phase in which you celebrate all of your efforts utilized in the previous four phases. You should be proud of yourself.

FULFILLMENT

Before reading further, please answer the following question: What does the term 'fulfillment' mean to you?

_____

_____

Fulfillment requires you to:

- Pat yourself on the arm, shoulder or back and say, 'finally!' Not so much because you have executed every single phase of this

chapter successfully but because you realize that you can envision your destiny and can see celebration on the horizon.
- Postulate yourself and determine if it was all worth it. Determine that your sacrifice mattered. Determine that your preparation was necessary. Determine that your planning phase was important to your strategy phase. Look back... now look at where you are currently and then look forward. Momentum is undeniable. Celebrate!
- Process the process. Take time to assess and evaluate if the end result is acceptable to you. What did you learn? Was it worth it?
- Prescribe your next steps based upon your current success. Are you willing to repeat the process all over again if you had to? Have others benefited and been strengthened from your experience?
- Pursue new adventures, new attitudes, new experiences, new life choices, and new endeavors. You are at a new place in your thinking... enjoy it. You are at a new place in your life... enjoy it. You are at new place in your finances, knowledge, and education... use it to develop your new character!

IN RETROSPECT

It's important to understand that this process requires a tenacity that can endure the nay-sayers and that can also endure the current economic crisis that the United States is facing. There are opportunities available for you. There are new relationships and business ventures that are available to you. A new and higher salary and personal growth and

...for the *College Grad*

development are all available to you. Do not limit yourself. Do not allow what you see to stop your upward, onward and continued progression toward who you want to become, where you want to reside geographically, and what you desire to contribute back to society. So look back...and smile. Look forward...and smile. Only you can limit you! I believe in you and I support your efforts as you continue on your road of *Preparation for Excellence!*

My Now...

...for the College Grad

Part 3: Future Success

My Now...

Dr. Kreslyn Kelley-Ellis

Life experienced first, then, academically trained - Educator, Entrepreneur, Trainer, Mentor, Coach, Community Servant and Activist.

Kreslyn left the field of education, to start her own business, Premier Leadership Academy. Her passion is still educating children, but now also includes educating adults. Her platform has moved beyond the school house, to conference rooms, auditoriums, and office space. Her subject matter has changed from reading, writing and arithmetic to leadership, diversity, character building, team building, goal setting, and helping others identify individual purpose and passion. Dr. Kelley's ultimate goal, is always to help anyone seeking higher ground realize that it is not only possible, but it is inevitable! Her simple, yet dynamic, approach is making herself real and transparent to others by sharing her own stories of challenges and triumphs. She is one of the featured authors of the book, *My Vision, My Plan, My NOW!* and *My Now for the Entrepreneur*.

For more information, visit her site, **kreslynkelley.com** or **placademy.net**.

...for the College Grad

If the Shoe Fits

Dr. Kreslyn Kelley-Ellis

It's the morning after graduation, confetti is everywhere, unwrapped gifts are dispersed throughout your car and bedroom, family and friends are headed back to their homes, and you may be still left with the question, "what's next"? In that moment and many more to follow, you begin to think of following up on submitted applications and resumes as you continue your job search, or if you're lucky, you are deciding which job to take. No matter which category you fall into, there are some things that every college graduate should consider above getting a job in their chosen field.

You have probably already been trained by your school counselors on how to search for jobs in your field and on how to properly answer questions during interviews. I would like to add that it is equally important for you, the interviewee, to be prepared to interview the interviewer in order to find the best fit for you. The way to do that is to first know yourself; your likes and dislikes, your priorities, your values and beliefs, your short and long term goals and aspirations, and then determine if the companies and job opportunities you are seeking fit your profile. You would never wear a shoe that is too small or too large, and feel comfortable wearing them. Well, the same is true in our professional lives. You only want to wear a shoe that fits YOU!

In the book, "Good to Great" the author, Jim Collins, tells businessmen and businesswomen to "get the right people on the bus, and get the wrong people off the bus." Do you think companies intentionally hire the wrong people? No, they hire people who they believe can do the job or who they perceive to be the best fit from the pool of applicants. People usually do not advance to the interviewing process without first meeting a set of qualifications or criteria. That pool of people can sometimes be too many to mention. Most interviewers do not ask enough exhaustive questions of applicants which pertain to their unique behaviors, personalities, ambitions, and desires to ascertain the fit to the position they are offering. Therefore, what often happens is, a few months or years after the hire date, the company may not be completely satisfied with you or vice-versa.

Though there is no exact formula, which can tell you whether or not you are a perfect fit, it is imperative, if you desire long term employment with the organization, that you: 1) know yourself, 2) have the freedom to express who you are with confidence and professionalism, and 3) ask the interviewer ample questions as to get to know them, their expectations, and determine whether they work well for you. It is always better to be the right person on the bus from the very start.

Being the right person or the right fit does not mean that you must modify your personality, unless of course, it causes you problems relating to and getting along with most people. Self-examination is pertinent to your personal growth if you desire to advance in any organization. Nevertheless, there are some things that hardly ever change or changing them takes an enormous amount of effort. They include...

1) <u>Your personality</u>

There is and will never be another person exactly like you. Some people are naturally humorous, while others are serious by nature. Some people feel extremely comfortable around lots of people, and some enjoy being alone or in small close knit groups. Some are global thinkers, and others work better with small details; and the list could go on and on. No matter what categories you fall into, you are who you are. Sometimes life's circumstances change a few characteristics, but many remain the same. What's important is that you know who that person is, and remain clear enough to be true to you and others about that person. It frees you to accept yourself and thus accept others who are unlike you. This process will provide you clarity in searching for a team, where your personality fits like hand-in-glove.

2) <u>Your life background and experiences (good and bad)</u>

As a child, there are some conditions both good and bad, in which you were privy to just because of who your parents and relatives are, the community in which you grew up, your friends, the schools and places of worship you may have attended, etc. As children, those things are usually chosen for us. Furthermore, for most, those experiences shape behavior through both acute and subtle ways throughout individuals' lives. It is important that you identify how these experiences have shaped you today and define whether or not the results of those experiences benefit you or not, especially now as you look to transition into the work place. If you discover you have good, healthy behaviors that fit well into that environment, then nurture those qualities. On the other hand, if you find that you have some behaviors that are harmful to you and others in the workplace, then they should be improved.

3) <u>The choices you made yesterday shape your today</u>

Any past decisions that have rendered a negative consequence today, fix it or live with it, as long as you are not making the same type of choices today. They can only haunt you if you continue reliving them. The rewards which have stemmed from good choices are where you want to continue to center your attention, and find other ways to make those choices and even better ones.

4) <u>Your gifts and talents</u>

You were born naturally talented in some area. You may have cultivated that area of your life and are considered the best at it by others, today. Then, you may have been one who did not need much practice or any lessons to manifest your gifts, yet you deliver them exceptionally well. Either way, this is a strong hint as to what you should do in this life, either in work or play. It is that part of your DNA that one should rarely if ever want to change, because it can serve you beyond your wildest dreams.

5) <u>Your desire and dreams</u>

...for the College Grad

Every child has inside of him or her a dream of what he or she wants to be when they grow up. Though experiences, discouragement, and the circumstances of life can seemingly snuff out those dreams, they are still down there somewhere. Almost everyone has a dream with a strong urging that leans them in the areas of service, like advocacy, justice, education, etc. Those passions exude themselves in different ways over time, but the root desire is usually still the same. Identifying those passions can help in getting to know yourself, reconnecting with your dreams, and can serve you well as you seek business and career opportunities.

This distinctive collection of talent, experiences, goals, dreams and desires gives you a shoe size unlike any other. You are a unique being; and as Susan Baroncini-Moe stresses in her book, "Business in Blue Jeans", be authentic and figure out the things that motivate you. Though this book was written for entrepreneurs or aspirants, these principles hold true when attempting to make a major life changing decision like choosing the right job for you, especially after thousands of dollars have been invested in your college career.

Baroncini-Moe also suggests that her readers write a mission statement for themselves. Knowing your mission helps to keep you on track to accomplishing it versus accepting a job because it pays more, it's convenient, or they are the first one that calls. Such actions could possibly take you further off track and eventually lead to the lack of fulfillment. Few people find luck when entering into a career with undefined goals, but most find it when they clearly identify who they are, what they want, and then work diligently to get it.

My Now...

Most people do not enter into a shoe store, while looking for the perfect shoe that goes with the perfect outfit, for the perfect occasion, and go straight to the shelf. They typically go to the sales person and describe, specifically, what they are looking for, the look they are trying to accomplish, and even ask for expert advice. If they do not find it there, then they go on to the next shoe store with the same mission in mind. You would do the same! Once you've found that shoe, you would study it, you would try it on and walk around in it, and maybe even compare it to a close match, just to make sure it is the perfect shoe and perfect fit.

Well, the same should be true when you are looking for that perfect position which aligns with your perfect personality, background, choices, talents, and dreams. You should literally interview the interviewer. This process is so much easier when you are extremely confident in yourself and you believe that it is your right to acquire the opportunity that best "fits you." Below, there are a few suggested questions to assist you in that process.

Possible questions the Interviewee can ask the interviewer:

1) What is Company X's employee make-up (gender, race/ethnicity, age range, etc.)?
2) What is Company X's mission?
3) What does Company X value most?
4) What are Company X's long term plans and goals?
5) How does one advance in Company X?

6) How much professional development does Company X provide to its employees? And, how are the development needs determined?
7) Does Company X provide a mentor to new employees?
8) Is Company X accepting of new ideas by its employees? If so, what is the process of sharing those ideas?
9) When and how does Company X evaluate employees? How is the information from the evaluation used?
10) If hired, what would be Company X's immediate expectations of me?

Of course, there are many questions that could be asked, but these will give a little more information about the company before you determine, when offered a position, if you really would like to start your career there. Again, I reference "career"; because, if you are just looking for a temporary job before getting fully into your profession, then this process may or may not be necessary.

Making a career choice can be one of the toughest life choices you can make, so it's important to consider what you really want. That may change five, ten, or maybe even fifteen years down the road; but, right now, get clear about what works for you. Self-awareness, self-acceptance, self-reflection, and devotion to self-development should be your starting point.

Align what makes you special with your educational background and skills set, and then determine what positions fit you best. This is will require ample research, because you must identify the companies which best provide jobs in the area you desire to serve and determine if they have a need for someone with your unique talents. Though this may seem time consuming, it will save you more time than when you seek out jobs, in which you are over or under qualified, that you really do not like, or that cause you to later realize you are on the wrong bus and have to go back to this process later.

Once you obtain opportunities to interview for the positions, which best suit you, you can confidently enter your interviews (just like entering the perfect event, with the perfect attire and perfect shoe), and own the room. You can freely express what makes you, you, what your strengths and challenges are, and share your skills, talents, and ambitions. Following the interview, when the interviewer or the interviewing committee asks, that popular question, "Do you have any questions for us?" you can humbly, yet assuredly, unload your list of inquiries for them.

This is just as much of a risk for you as it is for them. So, you have the right to properly suit yourself for your future. Therefore, after you are done interviewing with the numerous companies which now desire to have you be a part of their team, you can review your notes, thoughts, ideas, desires, and the pros and cons of them all, and boldly look yourself in the mirror and make a great choice once you've determined, "which shoe fits, and then wear it!"

...for the *College Grad*

Nabavi Oliver

Professionally, Nabavi Oliver is an Attorney, Consultant, and Public speaker. He has held progressive managerial roles and specializes in identifying inefficiencies, capitalizing synergies and helping organizations move forward. Personally, Mr. Oliver is an author and advocate for students' personal and professional development. Through his management of leadership programs and his mentorship of students ranging from middle school to post-college graduates, he hopes to inspire, motivate, and help cultivate our future leaders.

info@thepasgroup.com
www.linkedin.com/pub/nabavi-oliver/2b/965/50a/
NabaviOliver.com

...for the College Grad

Congratulations on Finishing: You Are Now at the Starting Line

Nabavi Oliver

It's not the end, it's the beginning. Each year, millions of students attend colleges and universities with an expectation to graduate. Without fail, many of those matriculants find themselves unprepared for adult life after graduation. Why is that? Why is it that some of our country's best and brightest are not ready to take on the real world outside of the comfortable and predictable confines of student-life? Is it because they are less intelligent than their counterparts? Maybe it's because the university system here 'just isn't what it used to be', and thus students are not workplace ready? Quite possibly, it could simply be laziness, right? Well, being a former college student and subsequent college graduate myself, I can admit there may be some truth to any of those statements. But is there something more?

We will start with a synonym for the term graduation – Commencement. Commencement literally means "the act of beginning". That is, the graduation ceremony is a time that not only marks the ending of a season, but also the beginning of a new one. It is a time when friends and family come together to congratulate on a job well done for a

My Now...

journey past, to impart gifts, love, and well-wishes for the journey to come. Graduation is the beginning.

If you are like most of us, this concept is one that you 'get', theoretically, but in actuality it may not fully register. We are familiar with the anxious countdown for our midterms and finals, noting how we'll never have to do 'that' again. We take pictures of each other and exchange our contact information, and fully intend to keep in touch with classmates. Ultimately, we are excited because we are done! But shortly after the goodbyes have been said, the gifts have been opened and the excitement turns into anxiety, we ask ourselves, "so what now?"

Much of the anxiety is because for the first time in years, we don't know what to expect. From our first day in organized schooling, which for many of us was kindergarten, we were being taught and groomed to follow specific orders on what to do, where to do it, and when. Throughout middle school and high school, though we are given progressively more responsibility on how we do the "what, where and when", those tasks were still defined for us. Then comes college, then graduation and somehow you are expected to make all of those years of following directions applicable to journey into adulthood. Allow me to be the first to tell you- calm down, this IS doable and you are doing most of it already. It is really a matter of taking responsibility for your failures and successes, working hard, and being purposeful and methodical about your goals. In this chapter, my hope is to make each of these tenants more tangible.

...for the College Grad

Subject Matter Expert, BS

You don't need to be an expert on anything but yourself. From that expertise is where you berth and sustain the confidence you will need to wow your interviewer, colleagues, classmates, etc. I know this is a novel concept, but consider it in its simplest form. When you are completely comfortable with a subject matter, it shows. Your posture improves, your voice has diction and emotion, you may even become comfortable enough to incorporate humor and heavens' forbid- smile. Now, think of the converse; to not be as well studied or prepared on material that you have to speak intelligently about. Your throat gets dry, your pauses in between thoughts are filled with "um's" and "ahh's". You avoid eye contact with anyone in the room for fear of forgetting the 2 points you actually do remember you are to speak about.

This is the first step to creating your brand as a young professional. It is like taking a test on a material that you wrote the book on. You are the subject matter that the employer is most interested in. So, give them what they want- YOU. It is not just the regurgitation of statistics and articles from the most recent journals that will speak volumes of your competency. It will be the way you find comfort in the grey areas. How you pause and are able to be candid and direct, yet humanistic and pleasant.

There was a new graduate who was ecstatic about an interview she finally landed. The day of the interview she showed up 11 minutes late. Sweat poured from her brow as she entered the office breathing heavily. In addition to being late, she had forgotten her resume. In a near panic, she called a mentor who gave her sound advice that made all the difference in the world. He suggested that she walk in with a chuckle and just be honest. She walked in, apologized for being late, and asked for a tissue to wipe her sweaty brow. Besides catching the wrong bus, she wore a black winter dress in the summer and accidently left her resumes on the bus where they were now getting a tour of the city. She explained that it was a start of a terrible day, but that it would surely turn around now that she has had a chance to express in person why she was the best (sweaty) candidate for the job.

While there was no guarantee that she would get the job she interviewed for that day, she certainly would not be easily forgotten among the other candidates. Her ability to keep her composure amidst interview catastrophe is what is referred to as emotional intelligence. Essentially, it is one's ability to control their emotions, yet still use them to make decisions about how to think and act. In the interview example above, the student was able to not only acknowledge her embarrassment and nervousness but also show her confidence in her ability to still be the best candidate. This is how tomorrow's leaders are being distinguished; your ability to see, feel, and respond in a professionally responsible way.

All of this plays a role in how you will be perceived which translates to your personal brand. Your level of comfort in knowing your strengths and weaknesses will have a direct impact on your ability to present your best you. In short, as said by author Ann Landers, "Know yourself. Don't accept your dog's admiration as conclusive evidence that you are wonderful."

Taste, Sample, Select

From childhood we are taught to put our best efforts into what we want to achieve. As we approach middle school and high school, the question of what you want to be when you grow up tends to shape your class selections, electives, extracurricular activities and even friends.

I start this chapter with an old sports story I am familiar with. Smaller than his schoolmates, a young boy sought out to stake his claim among his siblings and become the first athlete in his family. With his best friend a basketball phenomenon, it was easy for him to determine that basketball was not where his talent lay. He considered wrestling, but wasn't drawn to it. Besides, with size and body weight not in his favor, thoughts of being plummeted on a mat in front of his classmates were not the most appealing of visions. Having an affinity for running as a toddler and grade-schooler, he decided he would try his hand at track and field. The first day of practice his wise coach suggested all of the newcomers to the track team try out each event to determine if any of them had any natural talent that would show itself. The young boy, eager to find his niche lined up at the long jump pit. Letting out an audible grunt, he sped towards the pit of sand at full speed. He planted his right foot on the board, extended his body and stretched his legs to gain the most distance from his momentum. Despite his best efforts, he barely reached the sandpit. Long jumping was not for him. Next he would try his hand at the high jump and the 100 meter dash. To his dismay both ended with similar results. Next in line were the hurdles. As he approached, one of the seniors cleared three quick hurdles. His form was perfect, rhythmic, poetic even. They young boy took his place in line and finally it was his turn to try. The coach blew the whistle and he awkwardly took off sprinting towards this horizontal wooden bar. Wincing, he took a leap and hoped not to fall. After clearing the hurdle he exhaled and was startled by an eruption of laughter from the rest of the team. Apparently his hurdling form mimicked someone jumping a chain linked fence in a hurry. Not discouraged, and picturing the senior he watched moments ago, at that moment he decided that hurdling would be his event. He went to the open field, spaced out two hurdles and practiced jumping over them for the rest of track practice. The next several days were the same. Watching, learning, and implementing to perfect his form. His coach noticed his interest, dedication and willingness to come in early and stay late after practice. With that, his coach spent individual time with him, giving him tips and suggestions from his own past hurdling career. The young hurdler became more and more confident with practice and began to embrace the small cuts and bruises on his knee he gained from repeated hurdle drills and knocking hurdles over in practice. Though he didn't win his first race, or even his second race, there are some poignant lessons to be garnered from this story:

- There is truly a benefit to trying a few things out for size before you totally commit...shoes, ice cream flavors, even dating. I certainly would not suggest that anyone decide to marry the first person they go on a date with before the date begins;
- Just because it is the right fit, does not mean that it will be easy for you, that others won't laugh, or that you won't have to work hard for it. Famous football coach, Vince Lombardi said it best..."the dictionary is the only place where success comes before work";

...for the College Grad

- People help those who help themselves. The young hurdler's coach saw his dedication and chose to invest additional time and effort toward the young man's goals. This tends to hold true of parents, colleagues, mentors, and bosses;
- Dedication breeds reward- with more practice the hurdler became confident and it allowed him to accomplish more than what he initially felt possible.

Regardless of the electives that you have taken, the courses that you or your parents have spent a fortune on- there's no better way to find your place in the corporate or public sector world than trying it. Worst case scenario, you hate it and you can now cross professional cow milker off of your list. More important, however, is the best case scenario. When you find something that fits squarely in your sweet spot then you are able to excel much further than what you may have initially thought possible. Add in a helping of good-ole' fashion hard work and you can truly live up to your potential.

In case you were interested in how the young hurdler panned out, he had a full and beneficial athletic career. That same year he won a statewide competition naming him the fasted 16 year old hurdler in his state. He went on to gain interest from several Division I and Division II college athletic programs. In college he was offered an athletic scholarship, ran all four years, and with his teammates won the conference championship twice before college graduation.

My Now...

Demystifying greatness

Often, successful professional athletes, movie stars, performing artist, famous authors, and musicians are looked upon as being *lucky* to have such fortune as to *end up* rich and famous. People will even assume and prejudge why or how they have reached that level of acclaim. Maybe they had a wealthy upbringing instead of poor. They may have had both parents instead of just one, or belong to one particular race or have access to certain privileges that others may not.

The alarming truth is that these people are no different than any of us. They were all born with tools, gifts, abilities and shortcomings. However, we tend to set them on a pedestal, because to accept the truth that we too could achieve the same manner of success begs us to admit that we are not persistent enough, hardworking enough, or hungry enough to accomplish our goals and achieve our desires. Still aren't convinced?

Oprah Winfrey had a rough childhood filled with abusive relatives and alcohol use all before the age of 14. When she did land a job as a television reporter she was quickly fired because she was said to be unfit for TV. R. H. Macy's started but failed seven businesses before starting the successful Macy's retail store that is now world famous. Albert Einstein was said not to have spoken until he was 4 and was thought to be mentally handicapped as a child. Thomas Edison was fired from his first two jobs for not being productive enough, and was said to be too stupid to learn anything. Arguably the world's best basketball player, Michael Jordan was cut from his high school basketball team. I could continue, but I believe I have made my point. All of these individuals have left a legacy of greatness based on hard work and perseverance. So how do we demystify it? You must internalize that we all have our individual struggles, so what?! The question is 'how will you overcome them to be successful?' The only thing that stands in the way of your success is you. The first step is to take yourself seriously and take a proactive approach. My 4 step Proactive approach is to

1) Articulate (define) Your Goal
2) Plan a Realistic Approach
3) Implement Your Action Plan
4) Be Disciplined and Don't Make Excuses

I'll walk through this with a sentiment that many of us have heard to..."I want to be on time". We all can relate to being the first one at a meeting or event. You feel a sense of comfort in knowing you are at the right place at the right time. Alternatively, we can relate to being the late one to an event or a meeting. You are the center of attention, you interrupt the flow of the event, and people assume you aren't as responsible or you don't really care enough to be on time. That is not the image you want to portray to anyone.

Now, we will run through the four step proactive approach to accomplishing the goal of being more punctual.

1. For starters, let's articulate this goal.

My Now...

"I want to be punctual to class and work". We will define punctual, for our purposes to mean that we want to arrive to class or work at least 10 minutes early.

2. To plan your realistic approach, you must be honest with yourself regarding your habits, abilities, and lifestyle. If you know you are not a morning person and need three cups of coffee before you even open your eyes, you must account for this in your planning. This means going to bed earlier, waking up earlier or getting ready more quickly. Only you know which of these options work best for you. This step gets very specific, but once you get accustomed to it, it becomes second nature. The process should sound similar to this: I need to be at work at 8:50 am. Let's walk through your schedule backwards. My commute to work always takes 30 minutes so that means I must leave my house no later than 8:10 a.m. (always feel free to add in more time for cushion). I know it takes me about 50 minutes to 1 hour to shower, have my 3 cups of coffee, talk to my mom for 10 minutes and get dressed. So, I will set my alarm for 7:10 am. WAIT- I know I like to snooze at least 2 times, I will set it for 6:55 am to be safe. Although this may sound overly detailed, this level of specificity is what I would suggest to set yourself up to be successful.

3. Implement Your Action Plan. What time should you be in bed if you absolutely need 7 hours of sleep to function? Plan your evening accordingly in order to help you reach that goal. Move your night time activities to the weekends or make them after work activities if necessary. If you are a gym buff, workout right after work so that a late

workout does not have your body too wired to go to sleep at your allotted time. Lastly, go to bed!

4. Be Disciplined and Don't Make Excuses! This is where the winners are separated from the losers. You stayed up later than anticipated because your best friend and roommate needed to talk. Your alarm goes off and you feel like you just closed your eyes. Snooze once.....snooze twice... what do you do now? You DON'T think "I built in a 10 minute cushion, I'll just use that to snooze again". This is when you are truly disciplined, when you don't make excuses. This is a process that will become easier and eventually second nature. After the first few times, you will begin to see the benefit and appreciate the small sacrifices you have made to make you a better more punctual, you.

Although I cannot promise you that being punctual will bestow upon you Michael Jordan's athletic abilities or Oprah Winfrey's annual salary, it is a great step in the right direction. Taking this same proactive approach will allow you to navigate purposefully within your personal and professional life. It will garner you respect among your friends, colleagues, and bosses and give you credibility as the one who does what they say they will do. Lastly, it will provide you with a defined realistic approach to accomplishing any task.

My Now...

Pamela Glowski

Pamela Glowski is currently an Executive in a Northeast Ohio Staffing Service, a Life and Business Coach, Entrepreneur, Wife and Mother.

Pamela's expertise is in Sales and Marketing though she originally had a career in healthcare. Pamela started her own business in the travel industry in 2005. She was featured for her direct sales success in and Home Business Connection Magazine in April of 2006 and in Simply Home in their "Leading Ladies" Series in 2007. Pamela has developed proven strategies and has been a trainer and featured speaker in several Direct Sales Events including webinars, conference calls and live appearances. Pamela has created teleworkshops, group coaching sessions and offers One-on-One Coaching through her Life Coaching company Serene Insights. Pamela has used her training and coaching techniques to develop and grow her employers corporate sales team, many successful entrepreneurs, and looks forward to assisting you in "Creating the Life YOU Can't Wait to live!"

pamelaglowski@gmail.com

...for the College Grad

Work Ethic: What You Put In Is What You Get Out

Pamela Glowski

It's graduation day. The sun is bright. All of your friends and family have come to your college town to celebrate you and your achievements. You smile as you place your cap on your head, making sure the tassel is to the right side. You look at yourself in the mirror and you must be thinking, "I DID IT!" and you are right! You finished college!

The day was filled with photo after photo; you and your friends, you and your family, and you and your diploma. You are enjoying every minute of the festivities, including the graduation ceremony.

At the ceremonies you heard speeches from many people that you may, or may not, have known. You sat recalling many memories of the last four years as you heard much advice about how to be successful as you move into the next chapter of your life.

Your mind was swirling at this minute, thinking about your future, the possibilities, the new lifestyle you will lead, what you will be leaving behind, your friends, new friends you will make, where you will live, where you will work. There was so much to think about amidst all the excitement.

My Now...

During the course of the commencement ceremony, you were trying to absorb as much advice being given by the speakers, professors, administrators, family, and friends. Just as these sentences continue to string word after word, so do the quotes and useful tips.

In my profession, in the staffing and search industry, I meet many a new graduate who longs for the secret to success. In my opinion, the most important tip I can offer you is...develop your **WORK ETHIC**. It's not just about showing up every day.

Hopefully, you chose a profession that is centered on your passion and purpose. Now, everyone doesn't know their passion or their purpose, when they graduate, and that's ok. Sometimes passion and purpose are developed as you gain work experience and knowledge in your chosen field. You will naturally discover new avenues to pursue as you work. But you have to start somewhere.

When choosing your first job, choose carefully. Choose opportunities that align with your personal values. Choose opportunities that will give you the most learning potential for at least a 2-3 year period. This isn't an internship anymore; this is the beginning of creating your life.

Choose working environments you feel you are going to thrive in, where you will have training, support and experienced mentors who are willing to teach you what they have already learned and mastered. It's kind of like how you picked the college you would attend. Your workplace will be the next place you settle into in order to learn and grow.

...for the College Grad

You notice I didn't say pick the place that is going to pay you "TOP DOLLAR". Of course everyone wants to make the most money they can and that they deserve, but realize, you are just starting out. Some positions are just not designed to pay a great sum of money. Your experiences and potential continuing education opportunities could lead you to more income down the road. That depends on what your passions are and your ultimate goals.

Whether you chose your profession for the income potential or not, you have earned a college degree and that is a fantastic achievement. It's just the base knowledge you need to put yourself into the running for higher level and yes, higher paying positions...eventually. It's the first step in becoming an expert in the future. It's where you begin to make the ultimate impact and income you have the desire to achieve.

I am sure that after many hard studying nights and a lot of coffee, you must be thinking..."I have a great work ethic...If I didn't, I wouldn't have earned a diploma." That is true... in a way. You have learned how to learn in academia. You may have had short intern opportunities that introduced you to the "career" experience. Maybe you had jobs that required you to "be there" every day for the summer to help pay next year's school fees. If you worked full time while attending college, then understand that I acknowledge that you understand my next statement, but with your new degree, things are going to change in your work life, as well. Not to sound overdramatic, and grammatically incorrect... but, "You aint seen nothin' yet"! And that's a great thing!

My Now...

Years ago it was common for every teenager from about the age of 15 to have a part-time job, even in high school, or in the summers. If you did that, or worked full time while earning your degree, I think you are at an advantage, because you have "worked" somewhere. More and more, I see many people who are coming out of their college experience with no work experience at all. If you are reading this at a young age...work...whenever you can start. It's a good thing and it's your first lesson in "what you give is what you get". At that age, you get money, to be able to be able to afford dates, movies at the mall and "stuff" for your first car. It also is the first lesson in being recognized for achievements beyond school honors. It's a great feeling to know that your managers think that you do a good job. There's pride in doing a good job. It's also great to discuss in an interview later on.

Now that you have taken the classroom into the work place, "What you give, is what you get" has a whole new meaning. You aren't trying to just get a job to last you for a little while to get by. You are embarking on your career, which will mold decades of the rest of your life. How you work will determine how you will live, where you will live and possibly who you will live with. If you want to attract successful people, be one yourself!

In my role with the company I serve, I talk to businesses everyday as they are pursuing "top talent". What that means varies from company to company and hiring authority, to hiring authority. I have some companies that put great emphasis on GPA, some on extracurricular activities, but ALL of them want to hire those with a great **WORK ETHIC**.

From a hiring manager's point of view, they want to bring value IN to the company. They want to bring in honesty, good values, and strong judgment. Companies invest a great deal of money into new hires; in some cases, tens of thousands of dollars in training and resources in their first few months from date of hire. They want a return on their investment as soon as possible. This is what I mean when I say "What you take is what you will give back." Well, you kind of know what that's about if you have student loans from your parents or banks. You borrowed from someone to achieve your goal, now you have to do something in order to pay it back. That's part of good integrity, honesty and good judgment at this stage.

When a potential new hire goes in for an interview, the person or person(s) evaluating the candidate are trying to determine if the person before them is going to bring them the results that their customers expect. That's what they want in whomever they hire. So, yes, talk about what you have accomplished. Then relate it to how those accomplishments will be an asset to the company and their customers. Discuss how your education and experience thus far is going to support the goals and reputation of the company.

Don't think about asking about what you will get if you work for the company. You will find that out, if in fact, the company decides you are a front runner for the position. It's more important to see if you are both a match for each other.

The interview process is sort of like dating. It would be totally inappropriate for a girl to ask a guy on their first date, if he is willing to give her a 2 carat diamond with her verbal assurance that she will be a good wife. They don't know each other yet. They really have nothing more than words to solidify their potential for the relationship. In addition to that, it would be inappropriate for the same girl to scoff at a ½ carat diamond when the couple is just starting out. This example relates to salaries. If you are just coming out of college, chances are you will not command the same income with someone who has 3 years of experience. Remember, you can always build and go up with the right personal or business partners; and with the right **WORK ETHIC.**

Let's fast forward. You landed that first job! YEA YOU!!

Remember when we talked about the nights that you studied and all the coffee? Be prepared for that...again! Good **WORK ETHIC** includes taking the training period as serious as a college class. When you work 8-10 hours, plan on going home to spend 2-4 more depending on the company's expectations for your progress. You will be the first in, and the last out, each day. You may have to work on weekends to progress and to get better and better. Come prepared the next day with great questions and evidence that you learned something more than you knew the day before. Then keep reviewing that, applying it during the day, until you master it!

Now when in college it may have been customary to go to class, do homework, and then go out. NOPE...not now. You will want to get good sleep each night so that you can be at the top of your game. Please, especially take note of this if your career is focused on taking care people. Or at least this person anyway!

Coming into work dragging or hung over can be grounds for managers to think they didn't make the right investment. Or even dismissal. This also relates to your personal integrity and judgment. It isn't the image any company wants to project and no one wants to partner or be a co-worker with someone who can only contribute on a limited basis.

I seriously have had people come in on their first or second day already complaining how tired they were, that they didn't feel well, and nearly falling asleep in class sessions or while we were working on a project. My company can't afford that...and all the companies I know... can't either. And we don't put up with it. There are many recent grads who would love an opportunity and if it's not looking like the new hire is serious about their career, or getting the company to their goals, many will cut bait quickly. The college lifestyle was a lot of fun, but it doesn't work well in the working world.

Good **WORK ETHIC** includes connecting with those people who have achieved what you want to achieve; whether that's a manager, a trainer, or the president of the company. Connect with anyone who is willing to share what they have learned, their past and current approaches, tips and tricks...then give them the respect they deserve. You can't know more than they do, they are 3 years ahead of you in the journey. They can help you get to your desired level of success more quickly, and less painfully, than if you have to spend the time making all the mistakes on your own.

Most experienced managers, trainers, etc. are more than willing to help you if you are humble and don't have a "know it all" attitude. And they should be. It's part of their integrity, honesty and good judgment. They should realize that your success can have a great impact on the overall company's or organization's success.

If you don't take a "student" attitude, until you have some results under your belt, they can be very content to watch as you try to figure it out on your own, make mistakes, or even fail. I know that sounds harsh, but the stakes are high.

There are many great rewards to developing a great **WORK ETHIC**. It may be the home you are able to live in, the car you are able to drive, the monetary amount you can give to charity, the time you are able to spend with your family. With those rewards, count on times of sacrifice. The road to success is never easy. It's never a straight shot upwards. It's a series of ups and downs that require years of dedication. If it's what you truly want to achieve, you will work out a good work/life balance. The early years are the hardest because those are the years you are pushing the proverbial rock up the mountain. It's where you have the most to learn, the least to gain and the fewest choices. The more you build your expertise, the more you master skill, and the more you build your credibility and integrity, the more you will be afforded.

Just a side note...Work and life are never perfectly balanced, but it is simple science. "What you give is what you get; what you take you must return" is like that "equal and opposite" law. In my opinion, this "law" applies to everything. Here are a few "career examples":

...for the *College Grad*

1) If you give your best effort, you will be rewarded to the level you have delivered. If you want greater rewards, improve your efforts and skills.
2) If you ask someone to take their time to teach you something, return their kindness by getting a better result for the team, or offering to help when the same time is requested of you.
3) If you give someone a useful tip, get back a feeling of being able to share and being a team player.
4) If you use the Earth's resources, turn them into products that will improve others' lives safely.
5) If you put forth a good attitude at work, you will attract people who will support you.

You get it.

In a less specific and general way, there will be days when you need to do something in your personal life and your company will allow you to do it. That means you give the time back **before and after** you take off to tend to the personal business. There will be days when you will have to choose to give to the job. Perhaps you will be asked to pitch in on a big project and miss something that is happening in your personal life. It works both ways, and you have to make the decisions that are the best for the company, or best for your personal life, in each situation. Sometimes you may feel like you are giving more than taking, but trust me, it all comes full circle. On the flip side, companies do not hire and agree to work around you, your schedule, or your other obligations. You have to figure out how you will work your life around your work.

My Now...

Without work, you really can't have much of a life, so it's important to realize this fact of nature.

OK...back on track...Through the years you will make mistakes, you will fail in your personal and professional life. Stuff is going to happen. All your choices will not be the right ones. Life circumstances can change. Just make sure to fail forward, learn and NEVER QUIT... until you feel you have achieved what you were supposed to or needed to achieve, at this phase of your career. Yes, I said that correctly. NEVER QUIT... until you feel you have achieved what you were supposed to achieve or needed to achieve, AT THIS POINT IN YOUR CAREER. A Good **WORK ETHIC** includes knowing how to make a good career/life plan and knowing when to make changes.

This plan will start out looking one way, and change, several times, as you gain new perspectives about your career, personal life, family, goals and level of skill. Don't be afraid to make changes as you could actually delay your desired level of success or achievement by staying in the same place, for too long, for fear of making a change. Fear has held many a person back from reaching their true potential, so always keep developing personally, as well as professionally.

I was told by a great mentor of mine a long time ago that, "If I focused on developing myself, as hard or harder than developing my career, the success and results would follow". You will know when it's time to make a change. You will also know when you have made a change too quickly. Every time you are sensing a change, ask yourself, if your decision will be in alignment with:

1) Your Purpose?
2) Your values, morals and ethics?
3) Is this change what you want for YOU or what someone else wants for you?
4) Will the change give you the ability to improve your skills, talents and abilities?
5) Is it time to challenge yourself at a different level than you can achieve here?
6) Are you settling by staying?
7) Are you leaving because you are running away from what will really take you to where you want to be or running to it?"

A good **WORK ETHIC** requires us to be brave. Maybe you don't need to change where you work; maybe you need to change how you are working. Sometimes you may need to initiate change internally by standing up for what is right, just and for the overall betterment of the organization. Even when a recent grad is just starting out, they may have new, fresh, and GREAT ideas! Don't be afraid to share them when appropriate and when you have thought them through. Have courage to communicate what positive changes that can be made before jumping ship. Sometimes an organization is hiring recent grads for just that! Their creativity, the new techniques that they have been most recently offered in colleges and universities or maybe just the breath of fresh air they bring to a stagnant organization.

Being brave may also be deciding that the current opportunity no longer fits your career/life plan or the growth of the company. Think it through then make the right move.

My Now...

"Life is all about Choices and Chances...the Choices we make and the Chances we take!"©   Make the right choices, take the right chances and remember when it comes to your future career success, it's all about **WORK ETHIC: "What you give is what you get; what you take you must return!"**

...for the College Grad

My Now...

Andrea Foy

Andrea Foy is an award-winning international author, speaker, consultant and coach. She conducts workshops and seminars on topics such as: Women's Issues, Business Skills, Diversity, Image Consulting, Personal Success Strategic Plan and the Hire Power Series. Andrea is a Certified Professional Coach, a Certified Diversity Training Consultant and a Certified Facilitator with Moovin4ward Presentations. She is also an Independent John Maxwell Leadership Coach.

You can reach Andrea at **info@andreafoy.com** or visit her website at **www.andreafoy.com**.

Personal Branding: Achieve Your Full Potential!

Andrea Foy

People judge you in the first four seconds. They will then grant you approximately thirty seconds more before they make a final decision and store this judgment away in their subconscious mind. After that it is very hard for a person to change his or her first impression of you. And you never get a second chance to make a good first impression.

- Brian Tracy

You have graduated from college: Congratulations! You have had several years of studying, partying, sleeping, eating and wearing your pajamas outside of your dorm room. (We've seen you at the mall, airport, grocery store and banks.) Now those same people who saw you in public may be your future employers and like it or not; image goes a long way in your success in life now.

As a matter of fact, after writing my first book, *Hire Power*, I spoke to many HR professionals and business owners who lamented the casual dress and attitudes of some of today's job seekers, so this is an issue that needs to be addressed and now is the best time for you as the college grad to get your stuff together and wow employers and get that job.

Back in the day, your personal style was referred to as Image and it mostly consisted only of dressing for success, dress for the job you want, not the job you have, etc. Personal Branding is the new buzzword for how to appear polished, proficient, and professional. Nowadays with the advent of the Internet and the large social media domination, personal branding is a whole new and different concept, not just what you wear but how your 'social appearance' as well.

Let's look at both areas of your Personal Brand: Social and Physical. Lest you think personal branding is not that important, think of it this way. Employers and other organizations are more and more looking at social media habits of people they hire or choose to do business with. So if you don't manage or care what is out there you should. Big Brother is watching in a whole new way and it may keep you from getting that job, promotion, booking, gig, etc.

> "View your personal brand as a trademark; an asset that you must protect while continuously molding and shaping it. Your personal brand is an asset that must be managed with the intention of helping others benefit from having a relationship with you and / or by being associated with your work and the industry you serve." (Forbes.com)

So with all of this in mind, let's look at some of the more important things you need to have in order, in order to have a successful personal brand. *Dan Schawbel is the author of Me 2.0: Build a Powerful Brand to Achieve Career Success, and owner of the*

...for the College Grad

award winning Personal Branding Blog. On his blog, he has a toolkit of Personal Branding. I have taken some of his tools and added my opinion of their significance.

Professional Image

Business/Information cards

Make sure you have simple cards with your contact info on them. Not everyone has a Phone that can be IM'd to. This makes it easy to network or exchange info with someone you meet unexpectedly. Feel free to use the back side if you have a Mission Statement or something relevant to your life goal. The front side of the card should contain your picture and the following:

- Name
- Email
- Phone
- Educational degrees: MBA, JD, Dr. etc.
- Title: Author, Speaker, Coach
- Administrative Professional

> **ANDREA FOY**
> Author, Speaker, Coach
> www.andreafoy.com
> info@andreafoy.com
> (555) 555-555

Email

Keep in mind that emails is still used quite a bit in business nowadays. Many businesses still prefer to use email instead of social media. With that in mind, make sure you have a professional email. Sexygirl or Guyjock is no longer appropriate. If at all possible, get an info@andreafoy.com or andreafoy@gmail.com or something like that. The shorter the better.

When typing an email try to avoid stream of consciousness typing. Write it out first and the edit. Reread it. Do not use emoticons ☺; and your *signature line* should match your introduction card.

- Name
- Email
- Phone
- Educational degrees: MBA, JD, Dr. etc.
- Title: Author, Speaker, Coach
- Administrative Professional

Social Media

Social networking- more and more employers use sites like MySpace and Facebook to pre-interview potential employees. Be mindful what you post on them, especially pictures. The Internet is a new form of reference that speaks volumes about her personality and character.

Blog/Website

"If you blog, you need to own *yourname.com* or a website that aligns with your name in some fashion. Those who blog will have a stronger asset than those who don't because blogs rank higher in search engines and lend more to your expertise and interest areas over time." – Dan Schwabel.

LinkedIN

My experience with Linked in has been very positive, most of my connections for speeches etc. have been through this media. A LinkedIn profile is a combination of a resume, cover letter, references document. In combination with the groups that you have, it is a great professional asset to have. Seek recommendations and recommend others, join groups and network with them.

Facebook

Almost one billion people have pages as of late, but it still doesn't have the professional prestige of Linked IN. (Must be the animal photos!) Include a professional picture of just you, it should be the same as the picture on your business card, website etc. Nevertheless, input your work experience and fill out your profile, do not allow people to tag you in pictures and videos because they might find the pictures you do not want and post them. More and more employers are looking at Facebook as part of the selection process. You need to use a distinct background, don't forget to fill out your profile and include a link to either your blog or LinkedIn profile.

Twitter

Again same picture as the others. You need to fill out your profile and include a link to either your blog or LinkedIn profile. Be careful what you retweet and who you follow. Unlike Facebook where you can friend and unfriend, you cannot control who follows you as easily.

Video Resume

"A video resume is a short video of you talking about why you are the best for a specific job opportunity. You get about a minute or so to communicate your brand and are able to send the link, once you upload it to YouTube, to hiring managers." –Schwabel.

Bottom line, whatever media you use, you should have the same picture, try to use your full name only, no weird nicknames. Try to use the same color scheme and keep all contact info the same. The key word here is consistency.

Other Branding Tips

Resume/cover letter/references document: Even with all of the social media out there, at the end of the day you still need these documents that to apply for jobs and when you go on interviews. Do not use a generic resume for each position; customize each one you send out. Nowadays resumes are so much easier to do because you can use the online formatting feature. In the 'olden days', we had to format them ourselves and it was hard and very frustrating, retyping resumes over and over.

Referrals

Referrals: make sure people want to refer you! Let people know beforehand that you plan to ask them to refer or recommend you. You are being watched ALL the time ... and if you don't present a professional image during "off hours" that might influence someone about making a referral on their behalf. In other words, you need to be marketable and since people stake their own reputation on those they make referrals for, then they need to feel confident they're not going to create a poor reflection on them.

Handshake

Don't tie yourself into knots worrying about how to handle the handshake. The handshake should be firm, but not a hand-crusher—unless you're applying for a spot on the Worldwide Wrestling tour.

Offer your hand. Have you ever taken someone's hand and it was like driving a dead fish, limp. Subconsciously, a weak handshake translates a weak character. To project confidence, as you clasp hands, extend your index finger so that it touches the wrist of the other person. With a firm grip, shake three times and then released. Practice the *power handshake* so that it becomes second nature.

Thank you notes

Thank you notes set you apart from the others. They should always be written on good stationary and mailed. Do not send an email, handwritten stands out better. No matter how tech savvy we've become; an old-fashioned handwritten notes separate you from the crowd. You can find thank you notes and envelopes that match your rivers of the resume paper in stores like Office Depot. They are pricey, but worth it.

Buy them, address and thank them ahead of time. Before I interviewed for an administrative job, I brought thank you notes. On

My Now...

each one, I wrote "Enjoyed talking with you, I'm sure now that I would be an excellent fit at XYZ Company. I hope to hear from you soon. I then addressed them place a stamp on each envelope. After the interview, I went home, wrote in the names and mailed them within the hour. I got the job! It never hurts to thank people.

I attended a seminar where the presenter, said that her philosophy was to send thank you notes to everyone she came in contact with for networking purposes. She kept her business cards in a Rolodex in case she needed anything from advice to a job. Sounds like a good idea.

WARDROBE

Last but not least, what you wear is very important in establishing your personal branding statement. Appropriate dress in the working world still means getting reasonably dressed up these days, especially early in your career, but it is now harder to keep from crossing over the line from casual to sloppy because more and more companies are allowing more casual attire.

MEN

The essentials for men according to Gentlemen's Quarterly are:

1) 1. A Navy Suit
2) 2. A Grey Solid Suit
3) 3. The Classic Navy Blazer
4) 4. A While Dress Shirt: 100% Cotton
5) 5. Khaki Trouser

...for the College Grad

6) 6. The Tie
7) 7. The Perfect Polo
8) 8. Brown Shoe: *Shoes*
9) 9. Brown Belt: With silver buckle
10) 10. The Top Coat

It goes without saying but I will say it here:

Don'ts

- T-shirts
- Tennis shoes or flip-flops
- Sagging pants
- Jeans/cargo pants or shorts
- Earrings

Dos:

- Dress shirt and slacks
- Sports coat
- A belt and socks
- A tie is optional depending upon the position

WOMEN

The essentials for women according to Fashion for Dummies:

- Little black dress (LBD)
- Black blazer
- Crisp, white (cotton) button-down shirt
- Black trousers
- Knee-length black skirt
- Classic beige trench coat
- Black leather bag
- Quality blue jeans
- Pair of black pumps
- White and black cardigan sweaters

- Set of pearls
- Diamond studs . . . or cubics!

Don'ts:

- Stiletto heels, open-toes shoes or flip flops
- Skirts that hit above the knee
- Open or low cut blouses
- Flashy or noisy jewelry
- Wearing more than one pair of earrings
- Shorts

Do:

- Pants
- Skirts to the knee
- Sweaters
- Polos
- Button down shirts

Your Image Tells The World How To Treat You <u>And</u> How You Treat Yourself!

References

Fashion for Dummies, Wardrobe Staples Women Must Have among Their Clothing Items by Jill Martin and Pierre A. Lehu.

Job Hunting For Dummies, 2nd Edition by **Max Messmer John Wiley & Sons** © 1999 Citation

Forbes Magazine, http://www.forbes.com/sites/glennllopis/2013/04/08/personal-branding-is-a-leadership-requirement-not-a-self-promotion-campaign/http://www.forbes.com/sites/glennllopis/

Gentlemen's Quarterly, http://www.gq.com/style/about/ten-essentials

Schawbel, Dan, Personal Branding Blog.

...for the *College Grad*

My Now...

Andrea Jones

Andrea Jones is the founder and CEO of The Relationship Coaches.

If men are from Mars and women are from Venus, then Andrea Jones is definitely from Earth, providing a middle-ground perspective to men and women in both their personal and professional relationships with the other gender.

Happily married and the mother of identical twin boys, a teenage girl and a daughter in college. Andrea is also the stepmother to four more kids.

A native of Berlin, Germany, Andrea worked in leadership positions in mostly male-dominated work industries for over 15 years. For example, she was the one and only female business manager of a professional men's basketball team in Europe.

In 2000 Andrea moved to the States and created The Relationship Coaches to give women and men insights into the other gender, sex, and relationships that they might never get otherwise.

Andrea is a certified personal coach and corporate trainer, giving gender communication seminars in big corporations. Andrea is also the Executive Managing Director of the eWomenNetwork Chapters North Dallas and Northeast Tarrant County.

andrea@the-relationship-coaches.com

...for the *College Grad*

MENglish and WOMENglish
Andrea Jones

"How are you?" How often have you said this simple phrase within the last week? Now, be honest, did you *really* care every single time you asked how the other person was actually doing? Were you maybe even a little irritated when someone answered something other than "I am fine. How are you?"

Why is this important, you ask? Let me tell you a little tale…

Over 20 years ago, on my first visit to the United States, I was in a shoe store when the sales associate approached me and asked, "How are you?" I thought to myself, "*Wow*, she is really nice." My English was not all that great back then, so I was hastily trying to translate a decent response from German into English; however, by the time I was ready to answer her, the sales associate was already gone, talking to another customer. This entire process took only a few seconds.

Unfortunately, the sales associate did not know that I was a foreigner. My entire attitude towards the store and the sales associate changed immediately from "WOW, how nice!" to "It is unbelievable how rude this woman is. I am not shopping here ever again." Why? I'm German, that's why!

My Now...

I grew up in a culture where you only ask a personal question if you truly care or actually know and like the person. In Germany, a sales associate would ask "How can I help you?" rather than "How are you?" Asking and then not caring enough to wait for a response is considered unbelievably impolite. However, here in the United States, "How are you?" is more of a greeting than the beginning of a deep conversation. People are actually expected to say the phrase, without even thinking that it may be considered rude by others.

On the other hand, certain common German (or rather European) behaviors are considered discourteous and/or disrespectful here in the States. Let me give you a few examples:

1) If you ask me whether or not the dress you are wearing makes you look fat, be prepared for an honest answer.
2) It is considered socially acceptable to interrupt someone in a conversation. I will not wait until you are done speaking if I disagree or am not interested in the entirety of your story.

Different cultures, different rules, different expected behaviors.

What if I told you that men and women are basically from a different culture? Would that change anything about what you expect, consider appropriate behavior, or how you see the other gender?

Men are NOT "hairy women," and women are NOT "pretty, soft, multitasking, caring, emotionally unstable men." If you apply this principle in dealing with the opposite sex, your life will become so much easier – at home, at work, and even when applying for a job.

I am aware that it often seems to be politically incorrect to point out gender differences. However, **men and women are equal, but we are *NOT* THE SAME!**

Do not misunderstand me, I am not trying to take anything away from the wonderful progress and achievements that have taken place over the years, but acting as if men and women are the same causes problems both at work and at home!

Businesses and individuals have fallen into the trap of trying to negate the differences between men and women. However, men and women are different, in potentially powerfully and complementary ways. We are not trying to make life difficult for the opposite sex, but rather to coexist in peace without attempting to adopt masculine or feminine behaviors, or misinterpreting and judging the other gender. However, that seems difficult for most of us.

Men and women grow up and then live in different cultures with very distinct operating norms. In some cases, even different meanings for the same words exist. The appreciation and understanding of the differences will also lead to stronger connections in relationships with spouses, children, parents, family members, and so on.

You probably have the same sorts of questions that many of our clients had before they decided to hire us as consultants and become fluent in MENglish® and WOMENglish®.

1. ***Is gender really THAT important in defining the way people interact with one another?***

Yes, it is. You may doubt that gender is truly important in defining the way people interact and communicate with one another; however, the distinction between male and female is perhaps the most obvious, most visible, and most dramatic subdivision in our species.

An abundance of empirical evidence and theoretical literature documents differences between the sexes in behavioral realms, brain functioning, cognitive skills, peer relations, and hormonal makeup.

However, not all described behaviors and communication styles are exclusively used by one gender. Our training is based on numerous studies and we are concentrating on "the bell curve."

Again, these are not clichés, but researched-based findings.

2. **Are there individual differences as well as gender differences?**

Of course there are. Besides the demographic variables such as age, socioeconomic status, race, and cultural identification, there are also individual differences. You will find women that identify more with the male characteristics of communication style, and vice versa.

3. **How did men and women acquire their communication styles? Are we just born that way, or did we learn them?**

The old "Nature versus Nurture" question. Childhood lessons, gender expectations, *and* innate disposition influence how we talk and expect others to relate to us. Again, equal does not mean the same.

4. **Which communication style is better: male or female?**

No gender has the upper hand in communication. Both men and women have distinctive styles and bring forth a different perspective and skill set to the table.

The correct question to ask is, "Which style best fits the situation?"

The question that bothers me the most is this:

5. **Haven't things changed in gender relationships?**

Of course they have changed; however, we have not arrived! It is often assumed that after so many decades of women entering the workforce and climbing the corporate ladder that the gender problem at hand has been addressed sufficiently. The new requirement of corporate America is to have zero tolerance toward any communication inequities, such as ignoring women, hoarding both power and information, or excluding women from networks. But I repeat: Equal does not mean the same. Just because there are more female business professionals today does not mean that the attitudes toward them have changed. Men still dominate senior executive and CEO positions of Fortune 500 companies, and in many cases, make more money, even for the same job.

Outwardly, men and women know how to behave; internally, however, the same mindset still prevails, and attitudes will drive behavior.

A better understanding of innate differences and learned gender appropriate behaviors during childhood will lead to true equality.

Let's delve deeper into the behaviors and communication styles influenced by "nurture."

The gender socialization process begins the moment a child is born. The subsequent messages that individuals receive from families, books, television, and schools not only teach and reinforce gender-type expectations, but also influence the formation of self-concept:

a) Parents, family members, and friends discuss sex preferences for the unborn child before the first breath is even drawn.

b) The nursery normally does not get painted pink or decorated in the "Cars" theme until the parents know for certain what their child's sex will be.

c) Delivery room nurses hold and talk to newborn babies differently depending upon the baby's sex.

d) Parents ensure that their child has the culturally-influenced gender-appropriate appearance. For example, pink ribbons are placed in the few hairs on a nearly bald baby girl's head and the baby's ears are even pierced in some cultures.

e) By the age of two or three, children can accurately answer the question "Are you a boy, or are you a girl?" At this point in their lives, children adopt a gender just like they would an organizing characteristic, such as having brown hair or living on the same street. For a short time, children will also engage in mixed-gender play and dress. A boy might insist on wearing barrettes in his hair while a girl will refuse to wear a dress. Eventually, though, they abandon the gender behavior of the opposite gender.

f) By the age of five, most children have developed a fair amount of gender stereotypes. A boy might not approach a girl of the same age who moved in next door because he assumes that she wants to engage in "girls' play."

g) When entering school, most boys and girls will find themselves in a classroom with a female teacher. Over 75% of elementary school teachers are women according to the U.S. Department of Education, National Center for Education Statistics. (2012)

Correct gender identification remains a social norm. Gender ambiguity is considered distasteful. However, there seems to be a broader range of acceptable behavior for girls. A girl can be a "tomboy" while the entrenchment and rigidity of masculinity begins early, labeling a boy as a "sissy" or a "wimp" for gender unexpected behavior.

Reflect for a minute on behaviors that seem normal and expected amongst your own sex, but would throw you off if displayed by the other gender. Honestly, most of us are not even aware of how "programmed" we are. You may ask, "Why this is so important?" Gender expectations influence the way we relate to one another at home and at work. You can decide for yourself whether you want to (and will) change your gender expectations once you have kids of your own. However, you also need to be aware of the innate differences, as they explain behavior and communication styles and cannot easily be turned off like a switch.

My Now...

Gender expectation is one part of the puzzle. Now let's take a look at a few examples of how differently boys and girls play whilst growing up and how gender expectations manifest themselves more and more, or rather, turn into childhood lessons.

Boys

a) Rather engage in activity than in conversation.
b) Enjoy playing in large groups.
c) Most games have clearly defined winners and losers.
d) Elaborate system of rules.
e) Looking for status.

Girls

a) Most games are not competitive.
b) Looking for friendship.
c) Play in small groups.
d) Sharing of secrets.

<u>One of the different childhood lessons learned is...</u>

Boys have rules, look for status, and need a goal. A hierarchy is established, teams are built, and directions are followed.

Respect and competition are the main characteristics of boys' play. Conflict is part of the game.

Example: A coach tells a player to run 10 yards and make a right turn. The player will not question the order and will do as told.

Girls have no rules, status is not sought after, and the *process* is important. A flat structure is established, everyone has the same status, and the process will be discussed.

Relationships and their continuance are the main characteristics for girls' play. Conflict is to be avoided.

Example: One girl wants to play house, but the other wants to doctor. The solution is to bring the sick baby to the doctor.

As you can see, just this *one* childhood lesson heavily impacts what we consider as "appropriate behavior". For example, a husband says "NO" to his wife's suggestion to get a cat. His "NO" is now the beginning of a discussion for her, finding all the reasons why they should have a cat, while he is getting frustrated as he already voiced his opinion.

Tons more of these childhood lessons exist!

So far, we did not even touch on the innate differences, which, for example, explain why men can be content in sitting silently next to their partner for long periods of time, while women feel the need to communicate. Innate disposition also explains why women use more words to describe a situation and are comfortable multitasking, or why most men do not enjoy shopping for long periods of time and why they feel the need to come up with a solution for a problem.

Just turn on the Discovery Channel or watch Animal Planet. Do they ever say "There are no major differences between the male and female of animal X, so let's move on"? No. Every little detail is pointed out and discussed.

Humans are a species just like animals, and the innate differences are majorly significant. If you then combine the influence of "nurture" with innate differences you will start to understand why men and women, at work and at home, do not always understand each other, misinterpret, judge and even worse, use harsh words to describe the other gender. We are truly not trying to make life hard for one another; we just don't "get" the other sex and their behavior consequently baffles us.

The most valuable piece of advice I can provide for a college graduate is to truly pay attention to the differences between male and female and to not fall into the same trap as so many others do by negating the variances, just because it seems politically incorrect to point them out. Again, we are equal but not the same. If men are from Mars and women are from Venus, be from Earth and beat out your competitors with the realism needed to climb the ladder of success in today's society, regardless of your gender.

If you are able to adapt your behavior and responses to the other gender, without trying to act as the other gender, you will rock every job interview, be highly successful at any corporate job, build a thriving business, and have a happy and fulfilling relationship or marriage. In your next interview, rather than speaking English, remember the wisdom behind MENglish® and WOMENglish®.

...for the *College Grad*

My Now...

Michael Davis

Public speaking. Few phrases create more fear than those 2 words. It doesn't have to be that way.

For eight years, I struggled through embarrassing mistakes, confusing messages, and failed attempts to connect with audiences.

In 2001, a World Champion speaker taught me that world class speaking is a process that anyone can learn. If I did it, so can you.

I am committed to teaching others the world class communication skills I have learned. These lessons can change your life and help you accomplish more than you currently believe possible. My goal is for everyone whom I work with to gain clarity, confidence, and conviction in their communication skills so that they can Stand Out every time they present to others.

For more information, visit SpeakingCPR.com, email me at mike@speakingcpr.com, or follow me on Twitter: @Speaking CPR.

...for the College Grad

Increase Your Impact, Influence, and Income with the Power of Stories

Michael Davis

When I met my client Patti, she approached me at a Chamber committee meeting. A very elegantly dressed woman in her early-sixties, you could see she is a woman of means, with an uplifting and positive demeanor. But, something was troubling her.

"Michael, I hear you're a speech coach."

"Yes I am, Patti."

"Then I need your help. I made a **huge** mistake"

"What did you do?"

"Something really stupid, Michael…..I agreed to give the keynote address at the Women of Excellence dinner. I'm waking up sick every morning just thinking about it."

"Why?"

"It's not that I'm afraid to talk. My problem is, I don't know when to shut up! At our foundation, people are relieved when I'm done talking because I've finally stopped. I'm really worried that I'm going to embarrass myself and my foundation. I'm waking up stressed out, with knots in my stomach, like I'm going to throw up. Can you help me?"

The interesting part of Patti's story is that she wasn't scheduled to speak for another eleven….**months!** She was looking at the possibility of nearly a year of stress, anxiety, and morning sickness.

Jump ahead eleven months. Patti gave a speech three minutes *shorter* than her allotted time. She was funny, poignant, and evoked more than a few tears. And when she concluded, Patti experienced three positive outcomes:

She received a standing ovation.
People volunteered time to her foundation.
People offered money to her foundation.

What happened? How did she go from feeling **de**pression to making an ***im***pression?

She became a willing student of the art of speaking and storytelling. With these skills, she was able to present a speech that had impact and influenced the lives of others.

The skills and tools Patti picked up not only apply to keynote speaking, but also to one-on-one conversations, presenting to committees, and job interviews. Learning these skills can have a significant impact on your career because they help you appear more professional, more charismatic, and more influential.

By the end of this chapter, you will understand the foundational concepts of 3-Dimensional [or 3-D] Storytelling. You'll know why stories are a key component to communications; how to discover **your** best stories; strategies to make your stories memorable; and tools to deliver those stories in a dynamic fashion.

Before you learn the 3-D concept, it's important to understand WHY stories are so powerful. My friend and business partner, Jamey French says that, "Stories have been a connecting link throughout human history. Long before men and women invented writing, they passed down lessons through stories. 4,000 years ago, Aesop told fables that still teach us morals today. 2,000 years ago, Jesus used parables to convey his message. Today, stories have come back into vogue, despite the presence of *PowerPoint*."

Research shows that your brain is wired to learn through pictures and stories. You listen, you learn, and you reinforce lessons by sharing those stories with others.

A key to effective story telling is the emotional connections they can create with the listener. There are six common emotions you share with every other human being:

- Sadness
- Anger
- Happiness
- Surprise
- Disgust
- Fear

These emotions, generated though stories, connect with the visceral parts of your brain. Because the brain doesn't differentiate between real and imagined events, your stories can tap into the memories of other people. Properly told, your story will trigger them to think about their own experiences. This can cause the listener to relate to you at a deeper level.

For instance, in Patti's story, did you feel sympathy for her when you read about her daily physical reactions to simply *thinking about* giving her speech? Could you relate?

If you did, then you and Patti have made an emotional connection even though you've never met her.

Keeping this in mind, do you feel a reaction when speakers present facts and figures? Do these numbers stir your emotions and trigger feelings? Most likely, your answer is 'no', even if you can logically understand the speaker's point.

The real connection is made through the undefinable emotions your story conveys. What is meant by undefinable? Feelings that can't be defined in a couple of words.

For example, think about someone you love in a romantic way. Why do you love that person? In workshops, the answer I typically hear is *"Because he's good to me. Because she's beautiful. Because he is a kind person."* When I challenge them by pointing out that there are many people who are good, beautiful and kind, and ask *"Why is that one* person so special that you love him/her the way you do?" they finally give up and say, "I don't know, Michael. I just do."

And that's the point. Some feelings are un-definable. They just **are**. This isn't true only about feelings. Think about colors and sounds. Can you describe them? Think about the color red, or the sound of thunder. You can't describe them. Like emotions, they just **are**.

When you write your stories, share your emotional reactions, and the impact the story had on your life. Properly structured, your story will prepare others to receive your main message, the 'Aha' moment of your presentation.

Now that you understand why stories connect, how do you use the 3-D concept to develop and deliver stories that resonate?

The first D, or **First Dimension**, is the *Discovery* phase. To help you understand that your life is far more interesting than you believe, answer these questions:

Have you ever climbed Mt. Everest?

Won an Olympic Gold medal?

Discovered treasure at the bottom of the ocean?

Chances are, you haven't. Do you personally know anyone who has accomplished these feats? Again, chances are, you don't.

Although these people get notoriety, there's one problem with their achievements. Very few people can relate to them. They make for great tales, but emotional connection is tough.

On the other hand, have you:

Ever had a conflict with a spouse, friend, or child?

Struggled with deciding what to do with your life?

Faced financial difficulty?

Chances are, you have. These issues won't make you famous, or inspire a Hollywood movie, **but** they are relatable. These experiences can serve as a foundation for meaningful messages that resonate with others.

So which stories do you share? Those that taught you lessons or changed your life. By change, don't think major life-altering incidents that turned your world upside down. Consider more of the minor changes – such as beginning an exercise program, reading on a regular basis, or changing your listening habits to better understand the people you care about.

The following exercise has been a great help to my speech coaching clients. Create a Story File. On your computer, or in a notebook, list 3 columns. In Column One, write down every meaningful story from your life; in Column Two, list the lessons learned from each; in Column Three, write the long-term benefits you received from every one.

Column Three will be the one that connects with your audience, if the benefits you list are also important to them.

Column Two will be the foundational phrase behind each story. This is the message you want people to remember long after you have spoken.

Once you have your file, review the list to find the one story that has the most meaning to you *today*. Think about its impact on your life and how others can benefit from that message.

In my coaching practice, I share Patti's story because she represents a huge change - from literally being sick just thinking about speaking, to giving a presentation that compelled people to take action.

With your Story file in place, it's time to enter the **Second Dimension,** the *Development* stage.

When most people write a story, they start at the beginning, chronologically write out their tale, and conclude.

The problem with this is that your information is not centered around a single theme. This tends to diffuse your message, and leave people confused.

An effective formula for creating your story is the 5C Process. This consists of five steps:

1) Determine your key ***characters***
2) Create an escalating ***conflict***

3) Present the *climactic* moment
4) Share the *change* in your character[s]
5) Offer your *carryout* message

By describing your **Characters**, you create a connection with the audience because they feel as if they know these individuals. If they can relate to them, people will feel as if they are part of your story.

Once your characters are established, it's time to introduce **Conflict** to your story. This is critical because without it, there is no interest. Conflict can take on many forms - Person versus Person. Person versus Nature. Person versus a System. Person versus Him/herself.

In Patti's case, she faced internal struggles. Fear, uncertainty and lack of knowledge were making her sick. This threatened her peace of mind and the reputation of her and her foundation.

A key to effective conflict is to escalate it. Think about Patti's situation. She was anxious and feeling sick when I met her, and she faced increasing stress for nearly a year. When your conflict increases, it creates escalating tension within the audience. At the peak of this feeling, they're ready for the **Cure.**

This is the point in the story when the audience gets the 'Aha!' It is a change in perspective. They view their lives or the world a little differently. It is the essence of storytelling – the reason you tell your tale.

The only reason to take other people's time with a story is to change the way they think, feel or act. The cure step is the moment when you create that change.

Once the 'Aha' has been experienced, then the audience needs to see the **Change** experienced by at least one character. Since people often seek to improve their lives, they'll best relate to the story if a relatable change occurs that they can use in their lives.

For example, in Patti's story, she experienced at least two changes:

1) Whereas before, people were happy because she finally stopped talking, she received a standing ovation because her speech touched people emotionally.

2) She learned how to persuade others to donate their time and money in one speech.

These are typically the results sought by people who speak before groups.

These changes lead to the final step of the process, the **Carryout Message**. This is a phrase that relates to your main point. It's what people will remember long after they hear your story. When they remember your story, they'll remember your point.

A key to creating your Carryout Message is it's length. The shorter, the better. Some of the greatest marketing messages consist of a few words:

Coke is It

Where's the Beef? [Wendy's restaurant]

Just Do It [Nike]

Brief and pointed. These messages get to the heart of the message and convey to the listener the benefits they'll get by using the company product or service.

Another key to your Carryout Message is to not overload your audience with details. Many presenters provide so many that the people feel as if they're listening to a novel. With today's shorter attention spans, it's important to give just enough information to 'flavor' your scene, and get to the point.

When you effectively provide these 5 Cs of storytelling, you increase your influence, impact others, and inspire them to take action

Now that you have your story file and you've created the foundation of your story, it's time for the **Third Dimension** of Storytelling, the ***Delivery***.

Although there are many factors that impact your delivery, there are three critical ones that can help you stand out:

1) Being conversational. When you listen to most presenters, do they sound like they are talking in a conversational tone? Most don't. It feels as if they're either trying too hard to give a speech or they're so nervous that they look as if they'd rather be getting a root canal or standing in front of a firing squad.

To practice your delivery, tell your story to family at the dinner table, or when you're out with friends. This is an effective method to determine what resonates, which lines that *you* think are funny actually are, etc. If your tale passes the test with those closest to you, it's ready for an audience of strangers.

2) Moving with a purpose. Does this scene sound familiar? A speaker tells her story while prowling the room like a caged tiger. She moves from left-to-right, then right-to-left, traversing the room. For added entertainment, she holds a writing pen in her right hand and clicks it each time she stops and pivots to move in a different direction. This continues until you are lulled into a semi-coma.

What is the result of this constant movement? You don't retain anything the speaker says, and you may need to hit the coffee machine to make it through the rest of your day.

Unfortunately, this is probably the most common delivery mistake made by speakers.

What is the solution to this pacing habit? A common mantra in the speaking world is to *Move with a Purpose*. There are two keys to doing this:

One, break your story into sections that can be delivered from different parts of the speaking area. For example, when sharing Patti's story, I tell the part about her anxiety stage right [to the audience's left]; the part about her success is told stage left [to the audience's right]. This not only helps them compartmentalize each aspect of the story, but allows me to point back to each place on the stage and the audience knows immediately what I'm referring to.

An added benefit is that this creates a 'timeline' effect, and gives the audience a sense that they've been on a journey with you.

The second key is to know where to deliver your key points. Most people continually move around the stage while they deliver those points. However, to emphasize the importance of any key part of your story move to the center part of the stage, plant your feet, lean forward, and state your point.

This part of the stage is often referred to as the Power Point. [Please do not confuse that term, Power Point, with the *PowerPoint* presentation tool that every day puts millions of people across the world into a coma].

3) Using the power of silence. Of all the delivery tools at your disposal, this is the most important, misunderstood, and under-utilized.

Why is silence so important, and why don't most people use it effectively? There are two main reasons. One, most attempt to include so much information in their presentations, they quickly move from one point to the next, and leave no time for laughter or audience reflection.

From a delivery standpoint, when you speak too quickly and don't allow your audience time to laugh or think about your points, you're in essence telling the audience to *'be quiet.'* Would you do this in a one-on-one conversation? Probably not, if you want to keep your friends.

To maximize the impact of your message, do one thing at critical points in your story....Shut Up! Early in my speaking career, I was so concerned about what I was going to say that I forgot this rule. The audience would start to laugh at my humorous lines, but I'd cut them off. After doing this a couple of times, they stopped laughing.

Or, they would be interested in points I made, but didn't connect with me because they weren't given time to consider the implications. They became disinterested bystanders to my speech. Can you blame them? I was being rude.

The second reason for not using pauses is insecurity. Many speakers believe that if they aren't talking and filling the quiet space, they'll lose audience attention, because they'll start thinking about something else. The reality is, when you stop talking after key points or humorous lines, you allow them time to think about how that point relates to their lives. Or, you allow them to have a good laugh. This is where the connection is made. As my mentor Craig Valentine has said, *"The sale is in the silence."*

Remember, a presentation is a two-way conversation. The audiences' half of the conversation is their reflection. They may respond with a thoughtful *'hmmm'*, a nod of the head, a tear, or, a laugh. The effect is that you create a deeper connection, your story becomes an experience, and they remember your takeaway message long after you speak. However, if you don't allow that reflection time, the audience will mentally check-out. Wouldn't you do the same if someone continually cut you off in a conversation?

The best way to improve your presentation is to practice. Then ask for feedback. Make adjustments. Then repeat the process.

If you really want to improve, there is a fool-proof technique that will improve your delivery 10 times faster than anything. It is....RECORDING your presentation, and then watching it!

Chances are, you're first reaction to this suggestion is *"Michael. I can't do that! I **hate** the sound of my voice! I **can't stand** the way I look on video!"* This is a common response.

My response to that statement is a quote from one of my first speaking mentors, Darren LaCroix. *"Oh, you don't like watching yourself on video? Hmmm. Well, guess what? Too bad. **We** had to watch....so do **you!**"*

Although he delivered this in a humorous fashion, his point is well taken. When you see and hear yourself, you will quickly know why you get the feedback you're getting, and you'll speed up the process of correcting mistakes. If it works for world class athletes, actors, and speakers, it's good enough for you and me.

Congratulations. You now know more than most presenters about the foundations of storytelling, the 3D Storytelling formula. If you use these three steps to create and deliver **your** stories, then practice, get feedback, and make constant improvement, you, too, can become a World Class storyteller who impacts lives, inspires others to action, and accelerates your personal and professional growth.

I leave you with this thought. No matter where you live, or what you've done, always remember **you** have a story that someone **needs** to hear.

Books by Moovin4ward Publishing

My Now for the Entrepreneur: Motivation to Start Your Own Business

By Moovin4ward Authors

My Vision, My Plan, MY NOW: Motivation You Need to Take the Action You Want

By Moovin4ward Authors

Mapping Your Journey to Success: Six Strategies for Personal Success

By Sharon A. Myers & Mark W. Wiggins

Slumber Party, A story of four girls who pledge to survive high school and life… but don't.

By Sharon A. Myers

...for the College Grad

To book a certified Moovin4ward speaker to present a program, email speakers@moovin4ward.com

To purchase any Moovin4ward books in bulk (10+) at discounted rates, email books@moovin4ward.com.

www.Moovin4ward.com or www.Journey2SuccessPSSP.com.

www.ingramcontent.com/pod-product-compliance
Lightning Source LLC
Chambersburg PA
CBHW060513090426
42735CB00011B/2205